# TURNING P

THE CAFOD/ CHRISTI

LENT BOOK 2007

**Barbara Glasson • Pamela Hussey**
**Joyce Karuri • Moire O'Sullivan**
**Kathleen Richardson • Jane Williams**

# TURNING POINTS

Reflections on the
Scripture Readings for Lent 2007

First published in Great Britain in 2006 by

CAFOD
Romero Close
Stockwell Road
London SW9 9TY

Christian Aid
35 Lower Marsh
London SE1 7RL

Darton, Longman and Todd Ltd
1 Spencer Court
140-142 Wandsworth High Street
London SW18 4JJ

ISBN 0 232 52688 5

Note: the Hebrew numbering of the Psalms is used. From Psalm 10 to 147 this is ahead of the Greek and Vulgate numbering which is used in some psalters.

Cover photo: Annie Bungeroth, CAFOD
Cover design: Leigh Hurlock

Text designed and produced by Sandie Boccacci
Set in 9.5/13pt Palatino
Printed and bound in Great Britain
by Cox and Wyman

# Contents

# About the authors

**Barbara Glasson** is a Methodist minister in Liverpool city centre, working with an emerging church community that bakes bread. She trained in agricultural sciences at Nottingham University before studying theology at Nottingham and Hull. She is the author of *I Am Somewhere Else*, a mother, poet and a walker of dogs.

**Pamela Hussey** belongs to the European Province of the Society of the Holy Child Jesus. She has worked for the Catholic Institute for International Relations (now Progressio) for many years, and is the author, with Marigold Best of *Women Making a Difference*. She was awarded an MBE in 2000 for services to human rights in Latin America.

A graduate of St Paul's United Theological College, Kenya, **Joyce Karuri** worked in various positions in the dioceses of Mt Kenya East and Kirinyaga as theological tutor, director of communications, liturgist and hymn-writer. She edited the Anglican Church of Kenya's new prayer book, *The Modern Services*, and served as a member of the International Anglican Liturgical Commission (IALC). She is married, with a son, Alpha, 9.

**Moire O'Sullivan** worked for six years in Kenya with the Mill Hill Missionaries and The CRADLE, a local child rights charity; she is now Programme Adviser for Asia for Concern Worldwide in Dublin.

Originally trained as a teacher, **Kathleen Richardson** was ordained into the Methodist ministry in 1980. She later served as President of the Methodist Conference, Moderator of the Free Church Federal Council and President of Churches Together in England, and was made a Life Peer as Baroness Richardson of Calow in 1998.

**Jane Williams** is a visiting lecturer in theology at King's College London, and also teaches at St Paul's Theological Centre (SPTC) based in Holy Trinity Brompton, having previously taught at Trinity College Bristol. She is the author of several books, including *Approaching Easter* and *Approaching Christmas*. She is married to Rowan, who is Archbishop of Canterbury, and they have two children.

What is the point of Lent?

For Christians, it is the time when we try to trim away some inessentials, and return to and refresh the things that are at the real centre of our lives. What are the things that really matter? What sort of person am I – and what sort of person do I want to be?

So, we try to find a little more time to be still, to wait quietly. We try to let go of some of the less important things. We 'give something up'. We reach out to those in need, and in doing so we discover something of our own brokenness and need to be forgiven.

By making things a little simpler, a little less cluttered, we are able to see more clearly the things that are important. Love, justice, forgiveness, prayer.

But as Jane Williams reminds us in her opening reflection, Jesus insists that being 'religious', and doing 'religious things' are not the point of Lent. If we let them become the point, then we remain stuck in 'religion' and never discover God.

Lent can be a turning point in our life. We reflect on the gospel readings and their message of the sacredness of every human life and the blasphemy of unnecessary poverty and hunger. We live out these truths in our prayer and action. In becoming a person with prayer and the search for justice at the heart of our life we start to know God. And getting to know God is the real point of living in this world.

*Brendan Walsh*

# TURNING POINTS

THE CAFOD/ CHRISTIAN AID/ DLT
LENT BOOK 2007

# Jane Williams

## Ash Wednesday to Saturday after Ash Wednesday

*Ash Wednesday*

### A perfect excuse

Jl 2:12–18; Ps 51; 2 Co 5:20–6:2; Mt 6:1–6, 16–21

> *'Beware of practising your piety before others in order to be seen by them.'* (Matthew 6:1)

This passage has always been my perfect excuse for keeping my faith to myself. After all, if I go around telling people about it, surely it will be 'practising my piety before others'? I am more than happy to be the kind of armchair Christian that Jesus seems to approve of here, praying secretly, on my own, behind my own closed door, just God and me. A nice, private religion. Just what most of us have always wanted, especially if we're British.

Sadly, though, this approach only works if we resolutely ignore the rest of the gospel! This odd-sounding piece of advice comes in the Sermon on the Mount, where it is rather painfully obvious that the followers of Jesus are to be publicly identifiable. They are to be 'the light of the world' (Matthew 5:14), and even I can't persuade myself that that is best done in the comfort of my own home.

One of the underlying themes of the Sermon on the

Mount is about rewards. Starting with the Beatitudes in chapter 5, where certain kinds of behaviour are rewarded with blessing, Jesus is trying to get us to look at our motives. What does religion mean to us? Why do we do what we do? What is the hoped-for outcome? What do we see as the 'reward' of believing in God?

Matthew chapter 6 is a particularly good starting-point for Lent, because it is talking about prayer, almsgiving and fasting, all the things we should be concentrating on in Lent. But Jesus says they are not ends in themselves. Being 'religious' and doing 'religious' things are not the point, Jesus says. If we let them become the point, then we have got out of them all we are going to get. We have got the satisfaction of 'being religious'. But the real point of living in this world is to get to know God, and once we know God, we will long for others to know him too. God is the reward, the only one worth having.

So walking around with ash on your forehead is fine. It's not showing off, just showing God.

### Thought for the day
God is the point of believing in God.

### Prayer
Lord, give me such a hunger for you that I will never be satisfied with anything less. Give me a thirst for your justice that will only be quenched when everyone sits at your table and is fed. Give me a voice that will never be silenced until all your people stand before you together, in awe and joy. Amen.

## Profit and Loss

Dt 30:15–end; Ps 1; Lk 9:22–25

> *'What does it profit them if they gain the whole world, but lose or forfeit themselves?'* (Luke 9:25)

In a nutshell, Lent is about finding yourself by giving things up. So, in a sense, it isn't about discipline, but about self-fulfilment because, paradoxically, most of the things we think of as self-indulgent actually pay no attention to the 'self'. Most things that are marketed as 'treats' or 'pampering yourself' are actually about giving our bodies something either to relax them or stimulate them temporarily. A cup of real coffee, a nice glass of wine, a long soak in a scented bath, all of these things, we tell ourselves, are about giving ourselves a bit of quality time.

I've nothing against such indulgences – in fact, I'm writing this with a cup of coffee and a glass of red wine by my side, and my feet in a bowl of peppermint-scented warm water. But it is worth just mentioning that I am doing for my body what anybody – and I do mean any 'body' – would like. There is nothing particularly individual about this. No voyage of self-discovery is necessary to know that bodies like and even need stimulation and relaxation.

But only a rather more rigorous programme of 'self-fulfilment' will help me find out what my particular self needs in order to be satisfied, as opposed to what any old body likes. And that is part of the journey of Lent. What

4

is at the heart of our lives? What makes us feel most truly ourselves? What would leave us utterly bereft, if it was taken away?

The Christian answer to that is 'Jesus', but it is easy to say that when there is no danger that it will be put to the test. Jesus assures his disciples that that is the right answer. Only the God who is in Christ, reconciling the world to himself is worth everything. But do we believe that with our lives, as well as with our words? Lent is a time to find out, by giving up some of the props that we think we rely on to make us happy. We may be pleasantly surprised by our real 'self'.

### Thought for the day
It is possible that by giving up the things I don't need, I may come closer to the God that I do need, and so find myself.

### Prayer
Lord, you tell us to take up our cross. As we look around your world, we will see that many are struggling under the weight of poverty, injustice and suffering. Give us the courage to help to carry these crosses and as we lighten the load of others, give us the joy of knowing that we are walking with you. Amen.

## The Food of Love

Is 58:1–9a; Ps 51:1–5, 17–18; Mt 9:14–15

> *'Then the disciples of John came to him, saying, "Why do we and the Pharisees fast often, but your disciples do not fast?"'*(Matthew 9:14)

Jesus' attitude to food is one of the personal things that comes out from the gospel stories about him. He liked food, and sharing it with friends. He was critical of some of the food regulations of his people, or at least, of the attitude that went with them. He worried about the food needs of the crowds who followed him, and meals marked some of the most significant moments in his ministry, to the point where a meal becomes the characteristic activity of the Christian community.

This is not something that pious followers would have been likely to invent about Jesus, because it was clearly rather embarrassing. Serious religious people are supposed to fast, aren't they? John the Baptist was well-known for his ascetic life-style, and it added force to his message, because people could see his total commitment. Jesus and his followers, on the other hand, very conspic-uously didn't fast. Jesus turned water into very good wine; he ate with tax-collectors and sinners, to make them feel included; he fed the five thousand. What comes over is the picture of a man who was very good at enjoying himself, and whose followers had fun. It is easy to forget that, as the gospel story moves towards its dreadful climax at the cross.

But what underlies this attitude to food is the temptation that Jesus faced at the beginning of his ministry. After his baptism, when he went out into the desert and fasted, the devil came and tempted him to turn stones into bread. Everything that follows in the gospel stories shows that Jesus could easily have done that, and that he didn't think there was anything wrong with satisfying hunger. But when the devil tempts him, he refuses to make food for himself. 'My food is to do God's will', he says.

What nourishes Jesus is God, his relationship with God, his knowledge that he is loved by God. That's why bread and wine are the best means of demonstrating the love of God. We are showing what feeds us and keeps us alive, and we are making a place of hospitality for all.

### Thought for the day
God's food is the nourishment that is perfectly designed to sustain us and help us to grow.

### Prayer
Lord, teach us to trust that you really know what we need to feed us, so that we may grow into the joy that comes from sharing with you and all your people at the table of your kingdom. Amen.

## Patching it up

Is 58:9b–end; Ps 86:1–7; Lk 5:27–32

> *'Then Levi gave a great banquet for him in his house;*
> *and there was a large crowd of tax-collectors and*
> *others sitting at the table with them'* (Luke 5:29)

These little throwaway verses in the gospels, where Jesus
just goes up to someone and says, 'Follow me', and they
do, are actually mind-boggling. Whatever must Jesus
have been like, to have that effect? His presence must
have been extraordinary, and so must his insight into
people.

So here is Levi, sitting in his tax-office, surrounded by
people who feared and hated him in equal measure, and
yet despised him at the same time, because although he
had the power to take their money, they had the satisfaction of knowing that he had lowered himself to work for
the Roman oppressors, and that made them better than
him, in the end.

Jesus takes one look at Levi and sees a man in torment.
He entirely agrees with the other people's opinions about
him. He hates and fears and despises himself, too. Two
words from Jesus, 'Follow me', and Levi is free.

In the next scene, Levi is trying to offer that freedom to
others. What better proof is there of how good Jesus'
judgement of people is? Levi isn't trying to distance
himself from his past. Instead, he has invited all his old
cronies, the other outcast, wealthy, compromised tax-
collectors, to supper, to meet Jesus. He wants them to

have what he has found, the chance to start again.

It is so hard to believe in the possibility of a genuine fresh start. Whenever we think we have really turned a corner, we find we have actually just put a patch over a hole in our lives, but the basic fabric is unchanged. But it is much too frightening to throw the whole thing away and start again. We have to be as desperate as Levi before we can even contemplate such a thing.

Most of the people Jesus met didn't believe they were that desperate. Perhaps we don't think we are either. But the offer is there: don't patch it up, start again. That's Levi's testimony: it really is possible to follow Jesus into a new life.

### Thought for the day
If we keep patching things up, we will end up with something that bears no relation at all to the original.

### Prayer
Lord, I am so used to being ill that I hardly notice the cure you offer. Help me to reach out in trust and take what you are offering so freely and generously. Amen.

# Jane Williams
## First week of Lent

*First Sunday of Lent*

### Be Yourself

Dt 26:1–11; Ps 91; Rom 10:8b–13; Lk 4:1–13

*'One does not live by bread alone.'* (Luke 4:4)

I have only ever once been in the desert, and that was in Namibia. I saw the desert from the safety of an air-conditioned car, but even so, it was beautiful and terrifying, in roughly equal proportions. The source of both the beauty and the terror was the sheer alienness of the desert. It is absolutely not a place where human beings are in control. There is a road through the Namib, but the sand often covers it, and the dunes around change their contours as the wind shifts, so it is very hard to know where you are going. The landscape moves and ripples, and earth and sky are indistinguishable on every horizon.

So where better for Jesus to go to test his ministry than a desert? The chapters that follow after today's gospel are going to be driven by Jesus' authority, his certainty, his mission, his unwavering determination. But here in the desert, we see that all of that is based on something else. He comes to the desert, to a place where he is most obviously not in control, to find the force that will drive him. And that force is obedience.

The devil's temptations are very clever. He is only

tempting Jesus to be what he already is. 'Do a miracle, have authority, prove how much God loves you.' In the weeks and months to come, Jesus will do lots of miracles, and people will exclaim at his authority, and God has already told him, at the river of baptism, how much he is loved. So what harm can there possibly be in Jesus responding to these temptations?

But out in the uncontrollable desert, Jesus resists the temptation to be in control, to be the instigator of his own powers, to be the one at the centre of his own universe. 'Only God, only God, only God', he keeps saying to the devil. 'I am what I am because of God, not myself.' That's why this is the beginning of the new creation: because Jesus was prepared to be only what God made him, whereas we are always trying to make God be what we would like him to be.

### Thought for the day
Fear God and fear nothing else.

### Prayer
Lord, make us the people we are meant to be but can only be when we come together in your Son, Jesus Christ our Lord. Amen.

## The human face of the Judge

Lv 19:1–2, 11–18; Ps 19:7–end; Mt 25:31–end

> *'When the Son of Man comes in his glory, and all the*
> *angels with him, then he will sit on the throne of his*
> *glory'* (Matthew 25:31)

Someone once gave me a very good piece of advice: if
someone close to you makes you angry, remember what
it is about them that you love, then tell them off. I have
found this helpful over and over again. It doesn't stop
me from being angry, but it means that my anger is likely
to be properly directed at a particular offence, rather than
spilling out into some global condemnation of the
nature, features, voice, habits and very existence of the
person who has made me cross.

So today's gospel story of the sheep and the goats
starts with what might be reassurance, because the
person who is doing the separating is the Son of Man,
someone we know and recognize, who loves us; indeed,
loves us so much that he has voluntarily come to live
with us and share our lives. Surrounded by angels and
sitting on the throne of glory as he is, still it is his beloved
and well-known face that we see.

What's more, we understand his standards of judgment, because they are the same as ours. The judge isn't
suddenly going to reel off a whole list of strange by-laws
and sub-clauses that we have apparently contravened,
although we never even knew they existed. No, he is
going to look at the lives we have shared, as he has

shared ours.

But there the reassurance stops. Because Jesus' understanding of 'sharing' is not ours. We may share our lives with our family and friends, but not with the whole human race. It's all very well for the Son of God to think of 'sharing' in humanity in that all-encompassing way, but that's just not how we ordinary human beings think of it.

And then the human face of the Son of Man becomes the human faces of all those who have died of starvation so that we may have plenty, those whose countries have been ravaged by war so that we don't have to have war in our country, those who have been denied justice because we didn't care enough to challenge their oppressors.

### Thought for the day
God the Son came to share in our humanity, not just mine.

### Prayer
Lord, enlarge our vision we pray, so that there is room for all your people. Teach us that while others are diminished, we are too, and bring us trustfully to your judgement seat, hand in hand with all our sisters and brothers. Amen.

## Forgive us our trespasses

Is 55:10–11; Ps 34; Mt 6:7–15

*'Our Father in heaven'* (Matthew 6:9)

In the theological college where I taught for a number of years, the custom in that international community was for everyone to say the Lord's Prayer in their own language. I liked to shut my eyes and hear the wave of sounds, familiar and unfamiliar, washing over me and out into the world, to find their echoes in every place and every time that Christians meet. It is the Christian family prayer, one of the marks of our belonging, so familiar that it's hard to pay attention to what it is saying.

It is a prayer that has all the characteristics of Jesus' mission. It has the intimacy of his name for God – 'Father', and his willingness to include us in that intimacy. We dare to call God 'Father', although his name is too holy for us even to utter, because God's Son has told us to.

Then it has Jesus' longing for the time when everyone will do the Father's will, as he, the Son, does. After all, what else is God's Kingdom, but the time when his people honour and obey him? But we shall obey God not out of fear of his power, but because this King makes it his daily business to provide for the people. In God's Kingdom, we shall all eat God's bread, as the children of Israel ate the manna in the wilderness. There will be enough for all; more than the poor have ever had though less than the rich thought they needed. Jesus trusts God to be utterly dependable and radically just.

And then there is forgiveness.

How did the Christian church come to be such a judgmental place, when we only exist because of God's willingness to forgive? When we were still far off, before we even knew what we were looking for, let alone being able to ask God to forgive us, God met us in his Son and brought us home. This is the password, the essential characteristic – we are forgiven, and so we forgive. That's how we show the nature of our God.

### Thought for the day
Do as you would be done by, or as God has done for you.

### Prayer
Our Father in heaven, hallowed be your name. Your Kingdom come, your will be done, on earth as in heaven. Give us today our daily bread, and forgive us our sins, as we forgive those who sin against us. Lead us not into temptation, but deliver from evil. For yours is the Kingdom, the power and the glory, for ever and ever. Amen.

## A fishy tale

Jon 3:1–10; Ps 51; Lk 11:29–32

> *'The queen of the South will rise at the judgement with the people of this generation and condemn them, because she came from the ends of the earth to listen to the wisdom of Solomon, and see, something greater than Solomon is here!'* (Luke 11:31)

This chapter in Luke's gospel is one of escalating tension. Some people have said that Jesus' power, although it appears to be doing good, actually originates with the evil one. Then some well-meaning women, no doubt trying to pour oil on troubled waters, say, 'No, no he comes of good stock. Let's give credit for his powers where it is due – to his mother.' By the end of the chapter, Jesus is verbally lashing out at the local clergy and the lawyers, and making himself some very dangerous enemies in the process. And into the middle of this swims Jonah. What is he doing in this edgy, angry chapter? Well, I'm afraid he is up to no good. He may be a 'sign', but I don't think he's a good one.

Jonah is comically famous for being a grumpy and reluctant prophet. Everyone else in the story obeys God – the storm reacts to Jonah's disobedience; the fish carries Jonah to safety; the people listen and repent, even the bushes grow up to shade him when God tells them to. Only Jonah, God's chosen prophet, is out of tune with God. He does finally say God's words, but he doesn't want people to believe them.

Jonah's great sin is that he really did know God, but he just didn't like him. He wouldn't mind working for a God who was nice to his favourites but harsh and condemning to others. He just can't bear God to be just as prepared to forgive the people of Nineveh as he is to forgive his disobedient prophet.

So when Jesus tells his hearers that they are to take Jonah as their sign, it is not a compliment. On the contrary, he is suggesting that they, like Jonah, have God's words but don't want to share them. The queen of the south, the people of Nineveh, old uncle Tom Cobbley and all will believe in God and obey him before his own people do. Not much has changed since the first century, and the world is still very full of Jonah's. But we're not like that, are we?

### Thought for the day
I don't want to be a Jonah-sign, I want to be a resurrection-sign.

### Prayer
Lord Jesus Christ, help us to share what you have given us, so that we can rejoice with you over all God's children, ransomed, healed, restored, forgiven, singing with us the anthem of praise. Amen.

## First Thursday of Lent

### Say, 'Please'

Est 4:1–3, 5:12–14; Ps 138; Mt 7:7–12

> *'Ask, and it will be given to you; search, and you will find; knock, and the door will be opened for you'*
>
> (Matthew 7:7)

Jesus lived his whole life and went to his horrible death in radical trust in the God whom he called 'Father'. One of the things we are doing in Lent is trying to free ourselves from some of the other props in our lives to see how far we trust God ourselves. So we test ourselves by moving just slightly out of our comfort zones. Can we bear it? Is God still there? Very few of us test ourselves far before scuttling back to safety. Monks and martyrs may be called to more, but that is not the common vocation.

So Jesus' simplistic words in today's gospel reading are hard to take seriously. We do not intend to put ourselves in the position where it will matter much whether or not God will really give what we ask, or open when we knock. We will have God's provision for us as the icing on the cake of what we provide for ourselves. After all, we don't want to risk ending up like Jesus, do we? Look where his trust in God got him – crucified.

But all through the Sermon on the Mount, in Matthew 5–7, Jesus is trying to help people see what it might mean to actually believe in God, rather than just to pay lip-service to the idea of God. Supposing this really is God's world. Supposing the only reality is God's reality.

Supposing that all the day to day transactions that are so important to us – emotional transactions, social ones, financial ones, moral ones – are wholly meaningless. Only God is real. Everything else is a mirage. If that is so, then the only sensible thing to do, in fact the only possible thing to do, is to ask, search, knock until what you touch is the reality of God.

This doesn't necessarily mean giving up everything – though it might. But it does mean seeing everything with new eyes. Everything that is not God is transitory. It cannot save us or give us life. Only God is to be relied upon. What he is and gives, lasts.

### Thought for the day

Where your treasure is, there your heart will be also (Matthew 6:21).

### Prayer

Teach us to love everything that you give us, but always to love you more. Teach us to rejoice in possessing and in giving away, in comfort and in hardship, and in all things to look to you, our Lord and our Redeemer. Amen.

## Counsels of Perfection

Ez 18:21–28; Ps 130; Mt 5:20–26

> *'"But I say to you that if you are angry with a brother or sister, you will be liable to judgment"'*
>
> (Matthew 5:22)

The Sermon on the Mount, in Matthew 5–7, is enough to make anyone give up. This religion is just too hard. We prefer the Jesus who parties with tax collectors and prostitutes, and sits light to the finer details of the Jewish legal system. At least, we like that Jesus in relation to ourselves, though we don't really mind this stricter Jesus in relation to people who disagree with us. But the trouble is that there is no way of reading today's gospel as primarily a way of regulating how other people behave towards us. It is relentlessly personal, directed at each one of us.

It is salutary to think how much of religious life, how many religious controversies and schisms, are about our fierce desire to correct other people. Showing up others makes us feel self-righteous and reduces the need to examine our own lives. We know we're better than them – whoever 'they' may be.

But this passage is about us, and it is startling. All those little vices and grudges that we really hardly count at all are being laid bare for our examination. Surely God cannot seriously mean that as far as he is concerned, someone who is angry with another person is as bad as a murderer? Surely, thinking that other Christians are complete twits doesn't deserve punishment! This passage even says that the onus is on us if someone else is cross with us. Even if they are the offenders, we have to go and look for them before we can come before God's altar.

What we are seeing here is the way God functions. God does not hate or despise anything he has made. God runs out to meet us and put fine robes on us, even though we have ignored him or used him for most of our lives. We cannot make God be like us, but we can try to make ourselves a little more like God. It's always tempting to start that process by trying to change other people, but Jesus says in this passage that the only starting point is ourself.

### Thought for the day

Strange as it is, God likes my brothers and sisters as much as he likes me. I could try to find out why.

### Prayer

Spirit of God, teach us to love and forgive, not out of fear but out of longing for you. Teach us to study Jesus, to make him our model, even though we fail. Teach us to dislike our own faults but to look only for the good in others, and bring us at last into the likeness of Jesus Christ, our Lord. Amen.

## Wholly Holy

Dt 26:16–19; Ps 119:1–8; Mt 5:43–48

> *'Be perfect, therefore, as your heavenly Father is
> perfect'* (Matthew 5:48)

So now, this Lent, we have to be perfect. How likely is
that? It's the kind of statement that gives us the perfect
excuse not even to try. What is the point, since we have
no hope of achieving perfection?

Taken out of context, the instruction is daunting
indeed, and it doesn't actually get much easier when
seen in context, where it is talking about how the behaviour of Jesus' followers must exceed the normal
requirements of decent society. Anybody can love people
who are kind to them, but Christians have to love everyone. And we are not allowed to turn 'love' into a vague
and insubstantial concept, because the whole of the
Sermon on the Mount tells us exactly what love means,
in practical and terrifying detail.

But these verses are the clue, the vital insight into
God's understanding of love and perfection, and so,
presumably, of God's notion of holiness. God treats
everyone the same. God doesn't have favourites. The
goodness of God, his life-giving gifts and his presence,
are available for all, not just for believers. His sun shines
on all that God has created, because all that is created has
come into being through his Son.

And that is the 'perfection' that we are to aim for. We
are trying to learn to see each other and the world with

22

God's eyes, and this is the first and hardest thing that we have to get to grips with. We are called to see ourselves whole, as God sees us, and our wholeness is a collective thing. None of us can be whole on our own, because that is not how we are designed. We are designed to fit together, not to break up into little fragmentary individuals or like-minded groups.

Holiness, wholeness and perfection are related concepts in much of the Bible. The Church, like the people of Israel, is called to demonstrate, in our life together, God's perfect, holy vision of wholeness. That doesn't make it an easy Lent task, but at least it reminds us where our focus must be – not on ourselves, but on our common life.

### Thought for the day
Salvation is for sharing.

### Prayer
Lord, we pray for your Church throughout the world, that our life together may reflect your loving wholeness. Teach us to grieve at division, and to work for a communion that will give us a foretaste of your own perfect unity, Father, Son and Holy Spirit. Amen.

# Barbara Glasson

## Second Week of Lent

*Second Sunday of Lent*

### Look up

Gn 15:5–12, 17–18; Ps 27; Ph 3:17–4:1; Lk 9:28–36

> *He brought Abram outside and said, 'Look up at the
> sky and count the stars, if you can. So many will your
> descendants be.'* (Genesis 15:5)

Our hosts took us to the top of a local hill. It was dusk
and we were very new to India. As our eyes adjusted to
the quickly fading light, the group of Indian young
people coaxed us to gaze towards the crimson orb of the
setting sun. Huge and fiery it sank swiftly beyond the
horizon. From the tin roofs of sprawling and ramshackle
dwellings in the valley beneath us the last rays of the sun
glinted. 'Look, look at the sun' cajoled our proud hosts.
'How many people live down there?' asked one of my
UK companions. Should we look up or down?

In Liverpool, which is my home, the city seemingly
contradicts starlight with its own orange glow. We are
rarely able to gaze at the firmament, dumbfounded at its
vastness. I wonder if this is why experiences of the
'other' or 'the infinite' in our society are often sought by
artificial means?

Abram of course, that ancient tent dweller, had no
such dilemma, the moonscape and star shine of the
worlds beyond worlds, constellations, nova and nebula,

of seemingly endless scope, stretched him, and those ancient nomads, to the limits of their imagination and to the God who promised to relate to them. So, into Sarah and Abram's childless despair God speaks, 'Look Abram, look at the stars ...'

Look up.

After the transfiguration even the disciples had to descend from the mountain top and look down into the faces of the demanding crowd. But moments to look up at the stars, at the glories of a setting sun, to fill our minds with wonder are important reminders of the covenant connection between heaven and world. How else will we be able to come down to this struggling earth recognising the goodness of the Lord in the land of the living?

### Thought for the day

God of the heavens, help us to reflect upon the stars so that, when darkness crowds our vision, we will still recognise the lustre of your promise in the eyes of the people.

### Prayer

You, who has embodied for us
 a connection between heaven and earth,
be incarnate in our messy lives.
Wink your delight at us
from the deep sparkle in the eyes
of unlikely companions.
Lift our chins from our worries
and point out afresh
that the infinite embrace
of your love
is already sketched into
the universe.

## Second Monday of Lent

**You can't see the elephant**

Dan 9:4–10; Ps 79; Lk 6:36–38

> *'Do not judge, and you will not be judged, do not con-demn and you will not be condemned.'* (Luke 6:37)

I am sitting on an elephant. We have taken it in turns to climb up the back end of the kneeling Raja by virtue of holding onto his tail. Rickshaws, cows, motorbikes, cars, lorries, bicycles, pigs, women with babies wrapped with-in vivid saris, street children, all make allowance for our meandering progress, swerving to left and right.

From up here, I have the notion I could sort out this seemingly anarchic traffic – lights here, a policeman there. And why stop at traffic, what about the caste system, the birth rate and health care for the poorest? There is so much about being in India that has put me in touch with my inner fascist. When on an elephant, the one thing you can't see is the elephant.

Later we drive past the new call centres where our young hosts work night shifts for high wages. This need to telephone Europe and the US during our working days has profound implications for their Indian families. We pass McDonald's and a cinema showing *The Incredibles* and later the barracks which once housed the British Army. Globalisation, tourism, the balance between the rural and urban economies, colonialism, consumerism … these are some of our Western ele-phants. We can say, with Daniel, 'The shame now, as ever, belongs to us.'

26

Psalm 79 may help us pivot from despair to hope when the writer, also struggling with his personal and national failure, pleads with God, 'Do not remember against us the guilt of past generations; rather let your compassion come swiftly to meet us ….' The struggles of India may remind us of our collusion in multiple oppressions. But, if we are prepared to dismount from cultural certainties we might also recollect that God still takes the initiative on compassion.

Luke's ongoing challenge is both our caution and our salvation. 'Do not judge, and you will not be judged, do not condemn and you will not be condemned.'

### Thought for the day
Help us to possess the clear vision that comes not so much from riding high but from walking at street level with open eyes.

### Prayer
Monday morning God,
who sees the week ahead
with the clarity of timeless wisdom,
help us to climb down
from our assumed superiorities
of culture, education or money.
Lead us to contrition
as we realise
we have ridden our faith on the back of
too many conceits.
Give us courage to
live this week
without pretence.

## Standing in the gap

Is 1:10, 16–20; Ps 51; Mt 23:1–12

> *'Whoever exalts himself will be humbled; and whoever humbles himself will be exalted.'* (Matthew 23:12)

Often it is the simplest things that are the most moving. In the Aga Khan's palace, as we meander through the cool arches and whitewashed courtyards, we discover a cabinet containing Gandhi's staff and shoes. Gandhi suffered house-arrest and the death of his wife here. Amongst the gently irrigated lawns we almost stumble upon a low white stone that marks his modest shrine. The place is full of deep, uncluttered respect.

Jesus teaches his followers, 'Whoever exalts himself will be humbled – who ever humbles himself will be exalted', but humility and the pursuit of justice do not sit easily with our western lifestyles. Post-modern people are driven by the concepts of progress and individualism. We are much more likely to 'Make up heavy loads and pile them on the shoulders of others' – which in my native Scouse would be translated 'Do each others' heads in'.

In the first chapter of Isaiah people are called to the pursuit of justice, upholding the rights of the widow, the fatherless and the oppressed. The author challenges the powerful to relate in a different way.

In the Indian Methodist Church's leaflet on evangelism the question is asked, 'Who will stand in the gap?' Standing in the gap between the oppressed and the
28

oppressor calls us to put our bodies where our beliefs are – as Gandhi did. And as Jesus shows us, this is not just a comfortable 'option for the poor' but a radical reversal of human self-understanding.

Respect for Gandhi comes from seeing his integrity as he 'stood in the gap'. This is not superficial lip service to the notion of peace; as the psalmist reminds us, God desires the deepest faithfulness of our inmost being.

Standing in solidarity with the poor is a call to all people of faith. We are called to recognise that all humanity lives under the judgement and within the loving gaze of the same God. Standing in the gap, honouring the poor and challenging the ambitions of the powerful is a place of integrity – and it could cost us our lives.

### Thought for the day
The way of the crucified Jesus calls us to put our bodies where our faith is.

### Prayer
God of the pathway
be as close to me
as the shoes on my feet.
Mark my soles
with love for the poorest.
Bend my steps, lead me to less,
be my resolve
to journey extra miles
on this holy foot slog
for justice.

### An encounter with fear

Jer 18:18–20; Ps 31; Mt 20:17–28

> *'Is good to be repaid with evil, that they have dug a pit for me?'* (Jeremiah 18:20)

Some things are so terrifying that we lose the ability to be afraid. We entered such a collective moment when our minibus driver, who had speedily negotiated the mud tracks leading away from the village orphanage, decided to take a right turn onto the motorway. That is the wrong way up the dual carriageway. Apparently it was the quickest route to the petrol station.

'Oh God,' Emma seemed to be inhaling the words, 'we're all going to die.'

We dodged lorries, motorbikes and speeding cars that hooted wildly, swerving round us to left and right. What seemed like hours later, but in reality was probably only ten minutes, we stumbled out onto the dusty forecourt, rubbing our faces with sweaty hands and laughing uncontrollably.

Such a momentary encounter with our own mortality is a salutary reminder that for some this 'land of fear' is a daily reality. One member of my church community in Liverpool lives in a local wheelie bin to avoid kickings from passers-by or the arrest of police patrols exercising their 'zero tolerance' imperative. And in the Indian village we had just visited the orphanage marked a desperate response to the pressures of population and globalisation from within this isolated rural community.

Centuries before, Jeremiah questioned God: 'Is good to be repaid with evil, that they have dug a pit for me?' Political plots and personal circumstances have colluded to make fear such a daily reality for some in every generation. Survival may seem the most for which we can hope. Each day is a waking into new dilemmas, a fresh search for food or sanctuary or the relentless search to feed addictions.

In the conversation we overhear between Jesus, James and John in today's reading, we encounter the non-exemption clause in the gospels. Can you walk this path, drink this cup, be a servant? This is not a 'Be a Christian and get the best seats in heaven' agenda. It is the stark invitation to live without our religious security blankets. To drink the cup is to face our own death in the company of a saviour who is not saving himself.

### Thought for the day
Loving Lord, make us conspirators of goodness.

### Prayer
Because of the uprush of terrors
because of the litanies of grief
because of the excesses of tyranny
because of the intimacy of desolations
because of the derelictions of truth.
Stretch out your arms to us
Jesus, stretch out your arms to us.
Because we are only human
because we are only just human.

## Wake up!

Jer 17:5–10, Ps 1; Lk 16:19–31

> *'If they do not listen to Moses and the prophets they will pay no heed even if someone should rise from the dead'* (Luke 16:31)

The old men sit under the Tamarind tree. It is midday and heady with sunshine and the smell of spices. Poorly nourished babies are sleeping under the corrugated iron roof and the women are rocking them gently with one foot. Inside we stretch ourselves out under our mosquito nets. We rummage through our rucksacks and pull out our hidden supplies of throat sweets and muesli bars. We are glad to be away from the city's pollution – the fumes that clog our throats with black phlegm. We long to gulp cold clean water from our home kitchen taps.

The season of Lent ticks away minute by minute. Easter approaches. The world sleeps in apathy letting the waters of ecological disaster lap gently at its doorstep. We slumber through the imperative to see who sits in poverty at our gate. Where is God? Does he also snore like some absentee landlord sitting back on the haunches of creation? What will it take to convince us of the need to wake up to a new way of relating to the earth and the people of the earth?

Jesus the prophet, as Jeremiah before him, is an alarm clock for his people. 'Wake up and pay attention' he challenges. We need not be overwhelmed by wickedness. We can put our confidence in the God of heaven who is amongst the poorest. We can all be blessed like the tree under which the old men slumber but we need to share these riches. Then in exasperation he says, 'If they do not listen to Moses and all the prophets they will pay no heed even if someone should rise from the dead.'

The story of Lazarus is a jolt to open our eyes. Our earth and the people of the earth are under environmental judgment. We have slumbered under the nets of our own complacency for too long. The people are parched by our greed. What will convince us to change our ways? Even a man rising from the dead has not woken us. Wake up! Already the shadows are lengthening – imagine, soon even God could be hanging thirstily on a dead tree.

### Thought for the day
Bring us to our senses, Lord, make us conscious of the needs of each other and of the earth.

### Prayer
Take one hungry family
put into a tin hut
with some mixed messages
add only sufficient water to soak.
Leave to stand in a hot place
without stirring anyone to help.
Beat well.
Cover with anger
and a dusting of confusion.
Help us, sustainer God
to scrap this recipe for disaster.
Be content with simpler provision
and serve immediately.

### An investment in the unlikely

Gen 37:3–4, 12–13, 17–28; Ps 105; Mt 21:33–43, 45–46

> *'The stone which the builders rejected has become the
> main cornerstone.'* (Matthew 21:42)

The taking of malaria tablets soon became a communal
routine. Seven little pills through the week were soon
washed down with the hot sweet tea. But on Mondays a
huge bitter additional pill had to be faced. It was prone
to hit the stomach and make an immediate return. The
easiest way was to take it at bedtime and then lie flat.
One consequence was that it produced such alarming
dreams that the beginning of the week soon became
known as 'Manic Monday'.

Joseph was a dreamer. Hidden meanings were
revealed to him as he slept or day dreamed over the
sheep. His imagination brought him stories that were
interpreted as a gift from God. But dreams are not always
idyllic. They got Joseph into a cycle of jealousy with his
brothers and eventually into exile. Dreams may bring
unexpected joys or prophetic words but sometimes in
our sleep our fears surface. They can get played out with
alarming intensity and leave us feeling unsettled and
fearful.

God does not just operate on the surface of human
reality. He encounters us at every level, in waking, sleeping and the holding place in between, in the real face of
a passer by or in the unravelling of our assumptions, in
the need to share our bread or the transfiguration of

dominant paradigms. With God our lives can no longer be viewed from the sole perspective of self. That's why the idea of the stone the builder rejected becoming the cornerstone should not be a total surprise. God has a habit of turning our assumptions on their heads.

The good news is that, in the company of this covenant God, although we might be led to face our worst nightmares we are also continually surprised by split seconds of grace. We are blessed by being treated more justly than we deserve – and called to imagine how that can be for others in the unlikely risk taking of love.

Like Joseph, in our dreams we might face the abyss of our worst fears but also the euphoria of envisioning God's investment in the unlikely.

### Thought for the day
If you think God has a limited imagination – dream on.

### Prayer
Liminal Lord
who wanders on shorelines and challenges power
who touches the contagious and chides the seas
who draws lines in the sand and walks on the water
who honours the criminal and invests in the ill at ease,
help us not to cower on the edge of confusions
but imagine wider landscapes of love.

## Second Saturday of Lent

### The father who waits for us

Mic 7:14–15, 18–20; Ps 103:1–4, 9–12; Lk 15:1–3, 11–32

> *'But while he was still a long way off his father saw him, and his heart went out to him.'* (Luke 15:20)

The noise is both familiar and odd. It is the sound of a rock band practicing in a garage. It is a sound of home! But I am still in India, having a final walk round the dusty streets and passing a patch of wasteland where a pack of dogs sleeps through the hot nights. I am no longer surprised that there is a black hog scavenging in the skip. I have got the hang of 'being in a different world'. The rock group brings the realisation that this is the same world. And I want to go home.

At the airport there is a cow on the runway. The huge jet taxis carefully. We are soon high above Mumbai, where the tin roofs of the slums and the glass of the high rises glint their collective goodbyes.

What does the father see when the son returns? The father who has waited and watched the horizon, who has given his inheritance early, knowing it would lead to no good. What does he see as he raises the young man's bowed head, to look into the eyes of the one he has borne yet whom suffering has changed? Luke tells us, 'While he was still a long way off the father saw him and his heart went out to him.'

When we come home, whoever we are, home is never quite the same place that we left. We are reliant on those who have not shared the travelling to be patient with us as we try to describe the places they will never know.

The psalmist reminds us of God's patience with us in our homecomings: 'As a father has compassion on his children, so the Lord has compassion on those who fear him, he remembers how we are made, he remembers that we are but dust.'

Lent reminds us how God waits for us – waits in the struggling and the dereliction of words, waits in the span of the world, waits in the nonsense and mess. How our Maker scans the horizon, longs for us to appear again, small, vulnerable, dishevelled, but loved to death.

### Thought for the day
God has an infinite capacity to wait for us.

### Prayer
As the shepherd searching for a lamb
as the woman hunting for a coin
as the seeker digging for a pearl
as the scholar hunting for the truth
as the struggling looking for respite
as the hungry reaching out
so you call us home, dear Lord.
As a mother to her breast
as a father for his son.

# Kathleen Richardson

## Third week of Lent

### *Third Sunday of Lent*

#### Chosen

Ex 3:1–8, 13–15; Ps 103; 1 Cor 1:1–6, 10–12; Lk 13:1–9

> *'The Lord works vindication and justice to all who are oppressed.'* (Psalm 103:6)

We sat in a room in the 'lines' of a tree plantation in Sri Lanka. The other tiny houses were home to families, but this was the church. About fifty people, many of them children, were there to greet my sister and me. We had come from the UK to meet them. They sang and danced – and then demanded that we did so too! All we could think of on the spur of the moment was to sing, with actions, the song about Zachaeus being a very little man – which if you remember it, finishes with the words, 'I'm coming to your house for tea', which we thought appropriate.

It was the story of Jesus choosing the unlikely tax collector, despised by his neighbours, from whom to receive service.

We were then taken to another house in the lines to meet a family where the father had fallen from his roof and was paralysed. The small Christian community had taken it upon themselves to care for him and his family – turning him every two hours, supporting his wife, supplying the needs of the family from their own meagre resources. He asked us to pray with him and we then learned it was a Muslim family.

The readings today help us to think about God's calling, his choice of people to serve him. Moses appeared an unlikely choice as the one who would 'work vindication and justice to the oppressed'; the people of Corinth seemed unlikely candidates for sainthood; a failing and seemingly unfruitful fig tree in an illustration was not a likely thing to warrant further time and effort. And who but God could inspire an impoverished community to share what they had?

For God's choice of us is not according to our deserts or successes or strengths. He asks us to be willing to pause in our own activities to become aware of his presence; to let him change us from our selfish ways to become more like Jesus; and to be willing to allow him to work within us to produce the kind of fruit that will please him.

### Thought for the day
We are called to be a blessing to others – but in the process we are wonderfully blessed.

### Prayer
Lord, let me today be aware of your presence and willing to turn from my own concerns to consider if you are calling me to right some wrong. And reassure me again that where you ask me to work, it is your strength upon which I can rely.

# Third Monday of Lent

## Made whole

2 Kings 5:1–15; Ps 42 & 43; Lk 4:24–30

> 'There were many lepers in Israel at the time of the prophet Elisha …' (Luke 4:27)

She was ill, but had managed to keep it a secret, even to some extent on some days managing to deny it to herself. But the whispering started in the village where so many had died and she became the object of people's disgust and the subject of her own shame. She could deny it no longer – she had AIDS.

She was not welcome in her neighbours' houses and their children were told to avoid her children. The pastor came to her and said she should not enter the church since God had placed his mark of offence in her body. She could say with the psalmist, 'As with a deadly wound in my body my adversaries taunt me, while they say to me continually, "Where is your God?" '

Our readings today reflect similar situations. A Syrian commander is seeking to be rid of a disease that is a social disaster; even if he does not die from it, he is excluded from all other company. The remedy offered to him by Elisha is to associate him with what is alien to him, to bathe in the River Jordan, and to do so as a suppliant, not the general he was in his healthy state.

And when Jesus used this story to illustrate his good news of the Lord's favour he was speaking to those who prided themselves on their exclusive right to God's attention. He was giving an insight into the wideness of

God's concern that included the alien and demanded a similar inclusive attitude from those who would be his disciples.

But what is he saying about all those lepers in Israel? Did God ignore their needs in order to provide a useful sermon illustration centuries later? Where is God when so many are suffering?

I once heard a prominent surgeon say, 'I cannot heal. All I can do is to create the right conditions for healing to take place.'

We are called to be a healing community where those who suffer are held in compassionate relationship in the body of Christ.

**Thought for the day**
To be made whole is to recognise our significant place in the wholeness that is God.

**Prayer**
Lord, let me not despise the small things you ask of me today in the process of making me a whole person in the context of your world wide family. And give me the grace to offer to others the healing friendship of compassionate love.

**Forgive**

Dn 3:25, 34–41; Ps 25; Mt 18:21–35

*'How often should I forgive?'* (Matthew 18:21)

I was sitting in the class of six-year-old children in an
infant school on Friday afternoon. It was the custom in
that school to have Assembly at the end of the day and
on Fridays to give time before it to the consideration of
feelings and emotion. The teacher came to one little girl
called Violet and asked her, 'How are you feeling today,
Violet?'

The answer came, 'I feel really mad because my
brother threw a stone at my budgie and killed it.'

A little ripple of horror ran round the class. 'What are
you going to do about it, Violet?'

'Soon as I get home,' she replied, 'I'm going to kill his
budgie.'

Showing no emotion herself the teacher said,
'Children, if Violet does that there will be two angry
children. Can we think of any other way Violet could
deal with this?'

And the class of six-year-olds began to talk about how
to deal with negative feelings of hurt and anger. It was
deeply impressive. I tried to think if I could ever
remember an occasion when such a conversation took
place in a church group at which I was present. How do
we help people to consider more positive ways to absorb
hurt and resentment? At a time when conflict breaks out
in so many places, how can the witness and influence of

people of faith be significant? In the settling of accounts, particularly those that relate to the past, to whom should payment be made? When we seem to have just cause for resentment, who will plead our cause?

Azariah in the flames of persecution does not seek retribution, but asks God to accept a 'contrite soul' and a 'humble spirit', and the psalmist pleads for his own forgiveness – 'Do not remember the sins of my youth or my transgression – remember me'. Peter is told to forgive seventy times seven and later in that unforgettable and poignant moment in the High Priest's house when Jesus turned and looked on him, Peter remembered and wept bitterly.

### Thought for the day
Is it true that a soft answer turns away wrath?

### Prayer
Lord, forgive us our sins, as we forgive those that sin against us – and against you.
Let our anger be the righteous anger that confronts injustice with a positive alternative and not the personal vindictiveness that creates more conflict.

## Loved

Dt 4:1, 5–9; Ps 147; Mt 5: 17–18

> *'The Lord takes pleasure ... in those who hope in his steadfast love.'* (Psalm 147:11)

My daughter was nine and had to go into hospital for an operation. She did not feel at all unwell but something had to be corrected for the sake of her future health. I had to prepare her for what would be a very unpleasant experience. As we left home for the hospital she looked at me with tears in her eyes and said, 'If you loved me, you wouldn't make me go.'

How I loved her! But sometimes love has to be fierce and unyielding. Parenting which is too indulgent and has no discipline is often a failure in real love.

People who are suffering frequently express doubts about God's love in the same way. 'If God loved me ...' but I have also heard someone refer to 'The sweet iron of God's mercy.'

The readings today may not appear to be about love at all. They are about law, but law as the framework within which God is engaging his people so they can walk with confidence and continue to inherit the relationship he has established with them. So the writer of Deuteronomy says, 'What other great nation has a god so near to it as the Lord our God is whenever we call to him? And what other great nation has statutes and ordinances as just as this entire law that I am setting before you today?'

Of course it is not easy to keep hold of the great

intention of the just law without trivialising it into petty rules. It was a temptation into which it seems many of the religious leaders of the time of Jesus had fallen. But Jesus lifts the law before them as a great gift of God that he comes to fulfil, not to abolish. To be assured of a place within the love of God is not to be given a licence to do whatever pleases you, but to be offered the privilege of knowing what pleases God.

The psalmist shows his understanding of the law of God's love that is revealed in the seasons and patterns of the natural world with its long-term perspective and whole-world view.

### Thought for the day

Amid the disciplines of Lent, remember we are loved with an everlasting love.

### Prayer

Lord, let the scaffolding of your expectations about my behaviour and my attitudes keep me strong within the enfolding of your boundless love.

## Third Thursday of Lent

### Obedient

Jer 7: 23–28; Ps 95; Lk 11:14–23

> 'Do not harden your hearts ...' (Psalm 95:8)

The phrase 'It's like banging your head against a brick wall' occurs to me. Poor Jeremiah! He was reluctant anyway to become a prophet, and then he is told that the people will not listen. Earlier in the chapter (v 16) he is even told to stop praying or interceding for the people – though that is one command he seems to have disobeyed! At this point it seems the problem lies in the Temple. The people are wrapped up in their sacrifices and Temple liturgies to the extent that they will not listen to what God is saying to them. They call upon his name but will not hear the answer. They have substituted a form of service for the real service that God requires from them.

Psalm 95 has the same echo. It is a call to come to the worship of God and to recognise God's reign over them like that of a shepherd – but to do so as those who will then accept obedience to his voice and trust in his ways. The people cannot claim God's shepherding protection without willing obedience to his commands today.

Luke records a time when Jesus is accused of doing right things by the use of wrong powers. He has healed a man and his critics say his powers are those of an alien god, while others want a sign from heaven. Jesus responds by reminding them that it is God who sets free those bound by evil spirits and that this is a sign already

46

of the Kingdom of God among them. Spiritual discernment is needed to be able to see not just the outward action such as healing, but what it reveals of the purposes of God.

Paul called it 'holding the form of religion but denying the power of it' (2 Timothy 3:5).

In Lent we are invited to examine ourselves as those under authority. We must not hide under a cloak of religious observance or the claim to be the children of God. Obedience to the demands of the Spirit within is a requirement that may sometimes lead us into unexpected and unwelcome places.

### Thought of the day

We are not invited to a life where we may be comfortable and at rest, but rather to one where we shall assuredly be comforted and at peace.

### Prayer

Lord, in my Lenten observance, let me not confuse the form of discipline with the reality of a contrite and humble heart, and make me listen as well as speak.

## **Restored**

Hos 14: 2–10; Ps 81; Mk 12: 8–34

> *'You are not far from the Kingdom of God.'* (Mark 12:34)

I went at the invitation of Christian Aid to visit some of the projects in El Salvador which were supported by them. One day we visited a small, remote settlement where families returning from where they had fled to escape the civil war had been given a small plot of rough land. Christian Aid had provided the means to dig a well and had made it possible to have a teacher who came for two days each fortnight to teach the children. The well had just been completed and we were invited to receive the water from it and to bless it. Fortunately I was travelling with a Baptist minister who knew just what to do to avoid drinking the water! He poured it over his head and spoke of the blessing of belonging to God's family.

The hospitality they offered us from what little they had was another blessing. As we prepared to leave we asked if there was something they particularly wanted that we might be able to supply. We had thought they might ask for books, or food supplies but they considered together and came up with – 'a ping-pong table'. It was a wonderful moment. Here was a community that had so little but were moving out of bare subsistence and wanted to have fun together.

The readings today speak of restoration within the

purposes of God. Hosea, speaking out of his personal experience of hurt and pain, assures the people of Israel that God will restore them again to life and joy. The psalmist invites the people to shout for joy because of the promise of God to hear the distress of his people and to restore them to their place in his love. Mark tells in his Gospel of how Jesus sums up the law, linking irrevocably the response to God with the response to the neighbour. The scribe who had asked him the question is told, 'You are not far from the Kingdom of God.'

I wonder what Jesus meant. Bonhoeffer wrote, 'The Kingdom of God is not an ideal for which we strive, but a reality created by God in Christ in which we may participate.'

### Thought for the day
'Life can only be understood backwards, but it must be lived forwards.' (Søren Kierkegaard 1813 –1855)

### Prayer
Lord, disturb me when I feel content and complacent;
calm me when I feel anxious and fearful;
restore to me the knowledge of your abiding love;
and fill me with joy.

## Repentance

Hos 5:15 – 6:6; Ps 51; Lk 18: 9–14

> *'Have mercy on me, O God ...'* (Ps 51:1)

In the story of the Pharisee and the tax collector, if the Pharisee was telling the truth, and there is nothing to suggest that he wasn't, he had little for which to be sorry. He was a good, conscientious Jew, fulfilling the law and going the second mile. He was ready to thank God for it. Yet according to Jesus he went home without being 'justified' because he trusted in himself and regarded others with contempt. The tax collector, on the other hand, said he was a sinner – and again he may have been telling the truth! He however threw himself on God's mercy and, according to Jesus, received it. Humility and self-abasement open the door to God's mercy rather than self-righteousness.

Later Paul was to write that he too lived 'as to righteousness under the law blameless' (Philippians 3:6) but he had come to regard all his human achievements as rubbish in order that he could gain the righteousness that comes through faith in Christ.

It is a common mistake we make to think that to repent is to feel sorry for the things that we have done. It is much more than that. It is a radical turning away from doing what pleases us and turning to God. It is a change of direction that takes the person into a close relationship with God in faith, obedience and trust. Hosea tells most movingly of the restoration of that relationship and also sees that it is the work of God's grace within that enables the repentance. The psalmist on this occasion is said to be David, convinced by Nathan that his actions over Bathsheba were wrong and seeking both God's forgiveness and the power of God to enable the change of direction in his life. 'Create in me a clean heart, O God.'

Jesus on another occasion condemned some Pharisees for cleaning the outside of the cup leaving the inside full of greed and self-indulgence (Matthew 23:26).

Lent is a time for examining ourselves in the light of our Christian commitment, not just for the things we do that may not be consistent with our profession of faith, but more for our attitudes and opinions that may not be true to the Spirit of God within us.

### Thought for the day
What will we take pride in today?

### Prayer
Lord, let me not try to justify myself before you, and keep me from making hasty judgments on the behaviour of others. Assure me of your grace and mercy that receives all those who turn to you in humility and repentance.

# Joyce Karuri

## Fourth Week of Lent

*Fourth Sunday of Lent*

### Heavenly presence

Jos 5:9–12; Ps 35; 2 Cor 5:17–21; Lk 15:1–3, 11–32

> *'We are therefore God's ambassadors.'*
>
> (2 Corinthians 5:20)

Not too long ago, outside my business premises in a small rural town in Kenya, two weird-looking children, a boy and a girl, seemingly 5 and 7 respectively, passed by. Without the slightest care in the world and completely oblivious of the attention they were drawing, they went on to pick up here and there dirty macadamia nuts left over by the merchants. Without as much as wiping the mud off the shells, they picked up each small stone and then looked for a huge stone on which to crush their lucky find, much of whose inside stuff was mouldy or rotten. The pair grinned if it turned out to be good, and chewed it happily as they went on to try for some more luck. This was their lunch. And dinner? Who knows?

At that moment, I felt ashamed of the food on my table. I felt embarrassed at how there can be such poverty amidst plenty, and how we all move about and do our thing with absolute complacency, saying, in effect, 'It's none of my business.'

I remembered a single-parent family I had visited some time ago. They had not eaten lunch and had shared a single piece of avocado between them for dinner. When

I unloaded the goodies I had taken with me, so many other children had crowded around I nearly prayed for a feeding miracle. I introduced the elder girl, who was seven, to school. This morning she saw me for the first time in ages and called out, 'Joyce'! When I turned round she said, 'Wow! Wanja!' She smiled broadly and asked me to buy her a pencil, which I gladly did and she ran off happily to school.

We are Christ's ambassadors, making heaven a reality on earth, bringing down to earth heaven's values. The words of a familiar song come to mind: 'The time to be happy is now, and the place to be happy is here, and the way to be happy is to make someone happy and to make a little heaven down here.'

To be God's ambassador is to be like Jesus – seeing the image of the Father in all, stooping down from glory to relate with the tax collector, the outcasts, the wretched of the earth, lifting them from the dust of desperation and making for them a little heaven down here. When we act as such to any of God's needy children, we are lending to God. Someone said, 'Never look down on anyone except when lifting them up.'

### Thought for the day
May my heart be broken by the things that break the heart of Jesus.

### Prayer
Help me Lord to represent heaven on earth faithfully and shed abroad heaven's message of hope, love, forgiveness and reconciliation with you and fellow humans. Help me never to take for granted the availability of food on my table, for Jesus sake. Amen.

## Daybreak is coming

Is 65:17–21; Ps 30; Jn 4:43–54

> *'Weeping may remain for a night but rejoicing comes in the morning.'* (Psalm 30:4)

In 1984 it was the celebrated Kenyan film-maker, journalist and photographer Mohamed Amin who rang the wake-up call to a world that was sleeping to the reality of the massive famine in the horn of Africa, when his pictures showing the reality of the extent of the famine in Ethiopia were first broadcast. Like Thomas, we had to see with our own eyes before we believed. We saw the dead bodies of those who had succumbed to famine; we saw the strange figures of walking skeletons, the dying children and women, babies with hollow faces, sunken eye sockets and stick-like legs, clinging to their mothers' withered breasts for whatever drop of comfort they could find. I took some time to believe I really was staring at human beings made in the image of God. I wept loudly in front of the television. I was staring at a human catastrophe of great magnitude.

Soon emergency aid began to come in and there was some relief. Stories of famine can be moving and very grim. A woman had trekked an enormous distance with her two children before they succumbed to hunger only a few yards from the feeding station where she was taking them for high protein feeding.

War, famine and disease often seem to hit Africa with a harsher-than-normal blow, affecting life expectancy in a disproportionate way. It seems we often dwell in the dread of the night more than in the joy of daybreak. Yet, like an occasional episode in a general drama of pain, one day last year I had the joy of celebrating at a funeral of a woman who had died at the age of 115. Her husband, who had died three years earlier, had lived to be 119.

Yes, God wants us to enjoy our lives to the full, and to find fulfilment in every one of our days here. Anything affecting or interfering with this fullness of life goes against the wishes of God for us. Let us strive through God's help to be persons through whom Christ operates, to lead his people from the night of fear and anxiety to the daybreak of joy, seeking to enhance life in all its fullness to the greater glory of the Author of life.

### Thought for the day

No child of God for whom Christ died should die from hunger.

### Prayer

Sweep away every danger, every misfortune on the path of our life's pilgrimage, O dear Lord, that we may enjoy the blessing and wealth of long, healthy, happy and responsible lives. Amen.

## Enhancing life

Ezek 47:1–9, 12; Ps 46; Jn 5:1–3, 5–16

> *'There is a river whose streams make glad the city of God,*
> *the Holy place where the Most High dwells.'*
>
> (Psalm 46:4)

The Dead Sea is described as 'dead' because it receives, retains and evaporates. It never sends out. In personified terms, the Dead Sea is selfish. It loves receiving. And there are people and even churches that only receive and never give. Yet we read in the gospels that 'It is more blessed to give than to receive.' Remember: what you keep you lose and what you give you keep.

Being a Christian has everything to do with giving life, because we thrive in the rich soil that is watered by the blood of Jesus. Any tree that is not fruit-bearing will be cut away. 'You shall know them by their fruit.' This is why I believe that Christians must be at the forefront in lobbying for justice, peace and reconciliation in the world, so that all might enjoy life in abundance. Whatever little good you can do for a deserving person, you are doing it for the cause of Christ.

In the story of the healing at the pool of Bethesda, it beats common sense how a man can keep waiting for 38 years to be helped with that magical plunge at the moment it mattered. Luckily, he never seemed to give up even though it would seem that he might have waited for ever if Jesus did not pass by. His life up to that moment seemed to spell despair amidst hope, and he seemed almost to prefer to cling to despair even when asked a simple question by the Master healer: 'Do you want to be healed?'

Like the sick man at the pool, many people in despair seem to hold on to their familiar story of failure and frustration, and even to resist a quick solution. But lengthy stories of life's experiences can wait. Help must be given on the spur of the moment.

There are people all over the world, and people living close to us, who are living on the verge of despair, yet who are powerless to help themselves. Who will pass their way and give a word, or a helping hand, and be to them a fruit-full tree? What religious, doctrinal or other irrelevances could be standing in your way? As the great Bible teacher William Barclay once said, 'Human need must always be helped; there is no greater task than to relieve someone's pain and distress'. He added that 'Christian compassion must be like God's – unceasing ...'

### Thought for the day
Other work may be laid aside, but the work of compassion, never.

### Prayer
Sweet Holy Spirit, dwell in us deeply and lead us into the rich depths that Christ would have us reach in our understanding and practical application of his word. Amen.

## Fourth Wednesday of Lent

### Forgotten by God?

Is 49: 8–15; Ps 145; Jn 5:17–30

> *'Can a mother forget the baby at her breast? Though she may forget, I will not forget you.'* (Isaiah 49:15)

When I gave birth to my son Alpha nine years ago, he was a tiny baby who had suffered in the latter months of the pregnancy due to my high blood pressure. I was later to smile with satisfaction as I watched him grow from a tiny baby into a rounded, healthy and gorgeous boy. Does it break your heart to hear of Mums who throw away or kill their babies?

I read a story on the internet about a Puerto Rican woman who could not speak English yet wanted to assist in ministry in a difficult parish in New York. She would go to local neighbourhoods by bus to bring children to church and then take them home again. She only knew how to tell them, 'Jesus loves you and I love you.' After several months she became attached to one little boy. He came to Sunday school every week and sat on the woman's lap but never made a sound. Every week she would tell him all the way to Sunday School and back the only words she had learnt in English: 'I love you. Jesus loves you.' Then one day to her amazement the little boy turned around and stammered, 'I … I … I love you too!', then he put his arms around her and gave her a big hug. That was 2.30 on Sunday. At 6.30 that night he was found dead. His own mother had beaten him to death and thrown his body in the trash.

With so much to cause us pain and heartache, doesn't

it so often seem that God has forgotten us? How should we work our way out of what is for many a living hell? The answer is in our hands. Desmond Tutu once explained the difference between heaven and hell as follows. In both heaven and hell there were long tables loaded with good food, at each side of which sat people holding extra long spoons. In hell people were miserable; they were starving because they could not use the long spoons to feed themselves. But in heaven there was joy and laughter, everyone was healthy and not one was with want. The reason? They used their long spoons to feed those on the opposite side of the table. What a discovery! The long spoons were not for self-service but social service. Let's feed each other with acts of selfless love and kindness whenever and wherever need and opportunity may arise.

'I love you and Jesus loves you' were probably the last words the child heard in his short life from a Puerto Rican who could barely speak English. This woman gave her one talent to God, out of which a little child experienced love for the first time, even the love of Christ. What do you have to offer?

### Thought for the day

There is a mysterious yet very real way in which acts of kindness and generosity build for us a haven of joy and fulfilment that no amount of money can buy.

### Prayer

Lord, in your mercy help me to identify those near and far who bend or lie or walk in need of a helping hand, believing with the scriptures that whoever shows acts of kindness lends to the Lord, in whose precious name I pray and give thanks. Amen.

## Fourth Thursday of Lent

### A slide into Godlessness

Ex 32:7–14; Ps 106; Jn 5: 31–47

> *'Go down because your people whom you brought out*
> *of Egypt have become corrupt. They have been quick to*
> *turn away from what I commanded them …'*
>
> (Exodus 32:7f)

When my father died from a massive stroke in August 2004 my youngest brother was away and no one knew where he was, and not even news of our father's death brought him home. He resurfaced six months later. He has often been in and out of jail, real and civil, for he has been involved in all manner of petty crimes.

Surprisingly perhaps, the slightest suggestion of a change of character always brought much delight and beautiful smiles to my parents, who kept praying for him to be transformed. But their joy never lasted long, as soon everyone would start complaining of missing items which the boy would have taken and sold, usually for much less than their true value, for the price of a few mugs of some (illicit and filthy) local brew. My parents watched him with love and agony of spirit, and on and on they prayed.

Fathom our God and the lot he's had to grapple with since creation. Humanity has continued to love darkness more than light; we embrace easy religion that is self-serving rather than the life-giving gospel that demands our love, our life, our all. We love the prison of unlimited self service more than the freedom that comes with serving Christ. Today, we have dethroned God and enthroned self. Going to church looks archaic to many, while watching football and other sports has become an alternative kind of religion.

God is the same yesterday today and forever. What is he saying to us today? We have all sinned and fallen short of God's glory. Lent should be a time to repent and turn back to God because 'a broken and contrite heart he will not reject'. What is it that you and I have allowed to stand between us and Jesus' love?

Imagine the smile on the father's face when a wayward child comes home. Join me in giving God our Father lots and lots of enduring smiles as we return home and love him as we truly ought to.

### Thought for the day
They exchanged their Glory for an image of a bull, which eats grass.

### Prayer
The fire of your Holy Spirit is burning me deep, O Lord. Burn on, Holy Spirit, and purge me of all sin and unrighteousness, till my heart becomes your perfect dwelling place, and I a tool for Christ's noble use. Amen.

## Choose integrity

Wis 2:1,12–22; Ps 34; Jn 7:1–2, 10:25–30

> *'Let us lay a trap for the just man. He stands in our way, a check to us at every turn.'* (Wisdom 2:12)

Ever heard of 'New party mathematics'? The phrase was coined by the retired Archbishop of the Anglican Church of Kenya, David Gitari, in sarcastic reference to an incident of electoral corruption in the eighties in which, he said, 'The figure 5 is bigger than 500'.

What's the story behind this riddle? The enforced style of voting in Kenya at the time was that of forming a queue behind a candidate, a way of intimidating voters to rally behind the 'right' candidate until the one with a majority would be declared the winner. Often a political party would have chosen the candidate that it wished to see elected, and the rigging of elections would be their only way of achieving their goal. Such was the case in one voting station when a very unpopular candidate was declared the winner, although he had only five scared relatives behind him, while the other candidate had more than five hundred voters in the queue behind him. Bishop Gitari and the late Bishop Alexander Muge had visited this station on the day and had witnessed what was going on but they were chased away by scoundrels throwing stones. After their brave condemnation of the fraud, the church leaders heard the familiar cliche: 'Stick to the pulpit and don't get involved in politics.'

Sadly, many church leaders in my country have chosen

to remain silent in the face of corruption and bad governance. Why? Fear. Yet we read that 'God has not given us a spirit of fear but of power, love and a sound mind.' A year after his protest there was a politically-staged raid on Bishop Gitari's home. Had he not climbed onto the roof of his house he might not have lived to become the next Archbishop of Kenya. The following year, 1990, his colleague Bishop Muge died in a suspicious car smash. This was a moment of the imprisonment of truth, and the church leaders who courageously spoke out became much sought-after, their meetings thronged by all who loved the truth but who felt voice-less.

Shall we save our necks by appeasing wicked leaders, or shall we walk the tightrope of integrity, bringing honour to God? Those who walk the road of justice and truth may be conscious of the gallows of danger in their way. But the psalmist bids us to walk this road unabashed, 'For those who look to him are radiant, their faces are never covered with shame.' He further cautions that 'whoever of you loves life ... keep your tongue from evil and your tongue from speaking lies' (verse 12–13) because 'evil will slay the wicked, the foes of the righteous will be condemned' (verse 21).

### Thought for the day
'Evil is powerless if the good are unafraid.'

### Prayer
If integrity be like a piece of precious gold deep under heaps of useless rubble,
let me dear Lord be that gold. Amen

# Fourth Saturday of Lent

## A risky mission

Jer 11:18–20; Ps 7; Jn 7:40–52

> *'But, O Lord Almighty, you who judge righteously,*
> *and test the heart and mind, let me see your vengeance*
> *upon them, for to you I have committed my cause.'*
>
> (Jeremiah 11:20)

There is a saying in my language, *'ke guoya gacokagira nyina muigana'*, which bluntly translates as, 'A cowardly child returns to his mother whole.' The fighter, on the other hand, goes back with bruises, or never goes back at all. For a Maasai boy to qualify for manhood, he has to kill a lion on his own, armed only with a spear.

My heart reaches out to the mothers of all the brave young men and women who are fighting in wars in Iraq, in Afghanistan, or wherever. I cannot find the words to console those mothers who have lost beloved sons to war. And unless there is a sudden change of heart amongst those responsible for the conflicts, many more mothers will weep bitter tears.

Jeremiah suffered for being God's emissary, just as Jesus was hated though he represented God. There was no shadow of doubt as to whose interest they represented, and so they were bold to the end. Whose interests does war serve? Is it in the best interest of God and humanity?

Our countries' leaders do not always know what the right path is for the nations. They need the salt and the light of the earth, people of faith, to challenge them, to shake them if necessary out of their selfish, misled perceptions, and to declare boldly and with love: 'Thus says the Lord!'

But if we too are not to speak out of selfishness, we require the Lent discipline of prayer, fasting and self-denial, as we seek the face of God. He may not talk to us if our stomachs are too full and our egos bloated. And as God speaks to us, let us boldly speak out using every available channel and, maybe, someone will heed the message. Meanwhile, let us pray with all fervency for those who are sacrificing their safety for the sake of others.

### Thought for the day

Soldier, soldier, fighting in the world's great strife,
On thyself relying, battling for your life;
Trust thyself no longer, trust to Christ – he's stronger.
'I can all things, all things do, through Christ which strengtheneth me.' (*Golden Bells* 504)

### Prayer

O Lord my God, I take refuge in you:
save and deliver me from all who pursue me,
or they will tear me like a lion and rip me to pieces with
no one to rescue me.
O righteous God, who searches minds and hearts,
bring to an end the violence of the wicked
and make the righteous secure (Psalm 7:1, 2, 9 ) Amen

# Pamela Hussey
## Fifth week of Lent

### *Fifth Sunday of Lent*

#### A new thing

Is 43:16–21; Ps 125; Ph 3:8–14; Jn 8:1–11

> *'Go – and do not sin again.'* (John 8:11)

As we move nearer to the cataclysmic events of Holy Week, the liturgy of this fifth week of Lent opens with Isaiah's message of hope: the Lord, the Redeemer, will do a new thing: he will make a way in the wilderness and rivers in the desert, he will overthrow enemies …

In the Gospel reading we see Jesus in the temple early in the morning, teaching the people. The Scribes (experts on the Scriptures) and the Pharisees (experts on the Law) bring forward a woman caught in the very act of committing adultery, and, hoping to catch Jesus out, ask what he would do about her. Jesus, who did not come to abolish the Law but to bring it to fulfilment, tells the witnesses to cast the first stone, as the Law laid down, but he applies a condition: that the throwers should be without sin. He then bends down and writes in the dust. What did he write? An intriguing question, one possible answer being that he was listing the sins of the accusers. Jesus, in fact, has left nothing in writing – he is the living Word: word and action are one in him.

When the accusers leave, a short exchange takes place between the woman and Jesus, ending with his life-giving dismissal: 'Neither do I condemn you. Go, and do not sin again.' The sin is not condoned; the imperative 'Go', with surgical precision, separates her from her past and sends her out into a new future. She is no longer to be identified as 'the woman taken in adultery', but as one in whom God has done 'a new thing'. On Easter morning, Jesus will use the same imperative to another woman with a past, Mary Magdalen, 'Go to my brethren and say to them …' (John 20:17).

Throughout his life Jesus has reached out to those whom society has labelled and cast out, and restored them to wholeness and a feeling of self-worth. St Paul, once a persecutor of the church, also had a life-restoring experience and can say: 'Forgetting what lies behind, and straining forward to what lies ahead, I press on towards the goal for the prize of the upward call of God in Christ Jesus' (Phil. 3:13–14).

### Thought for the day
Am I ever grateful for the times God has done a 'new thing' in my life?

### Prayer
Father, direct each thought, each effort of our life, so that the limits of our faults and weaknesses may not obscure the vision of your glory or keep us from the peace you have promised. (Missal, Prayer for Week 3)

## Fifth Monday of Lent

### The cost of witness

Dn 13: 1–9, 15–17, 19–30, 33–62; Ps 22; Jn 8:12–20

*'The Father who sent me bears witness to me.'*

(John 8:18)

The key themes of witness and identity run through the readings this week. In the passage from Daniel, we see another woman, Susannah, falsely accused of adultery by two elders of the people. She is saved from stoning by the ingenious questioning of a young man, Daniel, which proves that the elders have given false witness.

The early Church was rich in witnesses (the Greek word is 'martus', martyr) who persisted in holding to the confession of Christ and were thrown to the lions as a result. Archbishop Oscar Romero of El Salvador is one of ten twentieth century martyrs whose statues now adorn the West Front of Westminster Abbey. Just two weeks before his death he said: 'I am bound, as a pastor, by a divine command to give my life for those whom I love, and that is all Salvadoreans, even those who are going to kill me ....'

In the gospel, Jesus speaks of his Father in terms of an intimacy, a closeness that mystifies the Jews, who were expecting another model of Messiah. 'Is not this the carpenter's son?' they had asked on hearing him speak in the synagogue (Matthew 13:55–57). His very ordinariness was an obstacle to their belief.

Pope Benedict XVI in his 2006 Easter Vigil homily reflected: 'The crucial point is that this man Jesus was not alone, he was not an "I" closed in upon himself. He was one single reality with the living God, so closely united with him as to form one person with him … His own life was not just his own, it was an existential communion with God, a "being taken up" into God …'

The meditations of John the evangelist open for us a window on the inner life of Jesus, a true reflection of his Father's being. Jesus tells us that to know him is to know his Father. When we see him arrested, humiliated, beaten, and crucified we can remember this.

### Thought for the day
Am I an 'I' closed in on myself?

### Prayer
Father, give us courage to speak with one voice and to work in Christ's name to bring your justice and fairness, your freedom and truth, to all your world. Amen.

## Fifth Tuesday of Lent

### Where was God?

Num 21: 4–9; Ps 101; Jn 8: 21–30

> *'I do nothing on my own authority but speak thus as the Father taught me.'* (John 8:28)

The Book of Numbers gives us an all-too-human picture of the people of Israel on their way to the Red Sea: God has saved them from slavery in Egypt, but here they are, impatient with the long journey and complaining about the food! We may have caught ourselves out in the same reaction: 'Why is this happening to me?', we often ask.

There is no easy answer – even Jesus on the cross cried out, 'My God, why have you forsaken me?' Pope Benedict XVI on his visit to Auschwitz in May 2006 asked the hard question, 'Where was God?' 'In a place like this', he said, 'words fail, there can only be a dread silence – a silence which is itself a heart-felt cry to God: Why, Lord, did you remain silent? How could you tolerate this?

Jesus in the synagogue of Nazareth proclaimed that he was anointed to preach good news to the poor, release to captives, liberty to the oppressed, sight to the blind (Luke 4:18). God is here, in Jesus, for all those, especially those on the margins, who recognise their frailty and their need. The passion of Jesus is truly the passion of God, in the two senses of the word: suffering endured, and the extreme of love. In Jesus, we see God acting.

When the Jews' questions continue – 'Will he kill himself?', 'Who are you?' – Jesus tells them that when they have lifted him up (as the bronze serpent was lifted up in the desert) 'You will know that I am he.' Today, when the crucifix is often demeaned by being used as a trinket, an adornment, dangling at the end of a chain, bejewelled, we could spend some time in prayer before it, reading in it the compassion, the passion of God, knowing that it images the salvation and the life of our world. A true jewel, beyond price.

### Thought for the day
'He loved me, and delivered himself for me.'

### Prayer
Father, open our eyes to see your hand at work in the splendour of creation, in the beauty of human life. Help us to cherish the gifts that surround us and to share your blessings with our brothers and sisters, and to experience the joy of life in your presence. Amen. (Week 17)

## The hard service of the Word

Dan 3:14–20, 24–25, 28; Ps Daniel 3:52–56, Jn 8:31–42

*'The truth will make you free!'* (John 8:32)

Daniel tells the story of the three young men who refuse to serve the gods of Nebuchadnezzar or worship the image he has set up, strong in the belief that their God will deliver them from the fiery furnace – and he does.

The fiery furnace in today's world is the price to be paid by those who refuse to serve the modern gods (read 'celebrities'), or worship the modern golden images, a price which can go from simple opprobrium and mockery, right through to actual martyrdom. Oscar Romero is just one example of those who were not afraid to speak the truth to power, especially the power of money, the root of all evil. He said in a homily in 1979, 'I denounce above all the absolutising of wealth. This is the great evil in El Salvador: wealth, private property, as an untouchable absolute. Woe to the one who touches that high-tension wire! It burns.'

Within weeks of his installation as Archbishop, breaking with tradition, he refused to attend official ceremonies until the terrible repression and death suffered by his beloved poor came to an end. Throughout his life he acted and spoke with the freedom of a true disciple of the Word made flesh. 'What marks the genuine Church,' he said in a homily in 1977, 'is when the word, burning like the work of the prophets, proclaims to the people and denounces: proclaims God's wonders to be believed and venerated, and denounces the sins of those who oppose God's reign, so that they may tear those sins out of their hearts, out of their societies, out of their laws – out of the structures that oppress, that imprison, that violate the rights of God and of humanity. This is the hard service of the word.'

Jesus' offer to the Jews of discipleship, truth and freedom falls on uncomprehending ears: membership of Abraham's race assures them of freedom, they think (the slavery they have actually experienced notwithstanding).

### Thought for the day
Identify your golden images.

### Prayer
Father, your goodness is beyond what our spirit can touch and your strength is more than the mind can bear. Lead us to seek beyond our reach and give us the courage to stand before your truth. Amen. (Week 27)

## The faithful God

Gn 17:3–9; Ps 105; Jn 8:51–59

*'Behold, my covenant is with you.'* (Genesis 17:4)

When God revealed his identity to Abram with the words, 'I am God Almighty' (17:1), Abram fell on his face. God changed his name to Abraham to mark his new role: '… for I have made you the father of a multitude of nations' (cf Jesus to Simon Bar-Jona: 'You are Peter, and on this rock I will build my church …' Matthew 16:18).

The covenant God makes with Abraham, and with us, is to last into the future – into eternity, in fact. These are tremendous promises, beyond anything Abraham could have imagined for himself. Abraham, for his part, and we for ours, must keep the covenant made with God.

'The book of the genealogy of Jesus Christ, the son of David, the son of Abraham' (Matthew 1:1). Now Jesus tells the Jews, 'Before Abraham was, I am' – using of himself the name given to Moses at the burning bush: 'Say this to the people of Israel, "I AM has sent me to you" ' (Exodus 3:14). There is no ambiguity about the claims Jesus is making about his identity, and it is this which leads to the charge of blasphemy. Non-observance of legal prescriptions could have been ignored, but to speak of God himself in this way is, for the Jews, blasphemy, and they take up stones to throw at him.

The evil in the human heart which will culminate in the crucifixion now begins to manifest itself – hands pick up stones. Jesus, the Word made flesh, used his hands to touch, to comfort, to heal, to offer bread and wine, to raise up, to wash the feet of his disciples. As Peter, telling the Gentiles in Caesarea about Jesus, put it: 'He went about doing good and healing all that were oppressed by the devil, for God was with him' (Acts 10:38). Those healing hands will soon be nailed to a cross.

### Thought for the day

Be thankful for the gift of our hands and the power of touch.

### Prayer

We pray in the name of the beloved Trinity that all the work and gestures of our hands may contribute to the building of the Kingdom among us. Amen.

## The prophetic voice

Jr 20:10–13; Ps 18; Jn 10:31–42

> *'Denounce him! Let us denounce him!'*
>
> (Jeremiah 20:10)

The terror to come is foreshadowed in the prophet's anguished words – but he can still cry out, 'Sing to the Lord, praise the Lord.' Jeremiah, like every prophet, felt compelled, almost in spite of himself, to speak the word in the Lord's name. Archbishop Romero, a twentieth century prophet and martyr, as he denounced the terrible repression suffered by his poor people, cried out, 'I, more than all the others, feel the repugnance of saying these things! But I feel it is my duty … simply to speak the truth.'

On one occasion, when he was going through the customs in El Salvador's airport, someone was heard to say, 'There goes the truth.' When he was told this, Romero said, 'That short phrase fills me with optimism, because in my suitcase I have no contraband, neither do I bring lies, I bring the truth.'

Romero was aware of the evil forces building up against him, testing his discipleship and his commitment to his beloved poor, to the limit. Already in January 1979, over a year before he was killed, he wrote in his diary: 'I was told this week that I should be careful, that something was being plotted against my life. I trust in the Lord, and I know that the ways of Providence protect one who tries to serve him.'

It is becoming clear now that Jesus will be arrested for blasphemy, 'because you, being a man, make yourself god.' As the net was closing in, Jesus went across the Jordan to the place where John was baptized, and there he remained. We can contemplate him as he sits by the Jordan where he received the baptism of John, where the Spirit descended upon him, and where he heard the voice from heaven telling him he was the beloved Son. We can imagine that he gathered strength from this memory.

### Thought for the day
Consider the cost for me, here and now, of Christian witness.

### Prayer
Father, form in us the likeness of your Son. Send us as witnesses of gospel truth into a world of fragile peace and broken promises, and strengthen us in our active love for the poor ones of our world. Amen (Week 8)

## The gathering clouds

Ezk 37:21–28; Jer 31:10–13; Jn 11:45–57

> *'They shall be my people, and I will be their God.'*
> (Ezekiel 37:23)

. As the storm clouds gather we need to be strengthened in our faith and hope: so the liturgy puts before us the promises of the faithful God. God will take them, gather them, bring them, save them, cleanse them – the verbs tumble over each other till they reach their climax: 'and they shall be my people, and I will be their God.'

Pope Benedict XVI on his visit to Auschwitz commented that the Nazis' Final Solution was an attack on the One God himself, by attempting to root out the people who carried his message. 'Deep down ... those vicious criminals, by wiping out this people, wanted to kill the God who called Abraham, who spoke on Sinai and laid down principles to serve as a guide for mankind, principles that are eternally valid. If this people, by its very existence, was a witness to the God who spoke to humanity and took us to himself, then that God finally had to die and power had to belong to man alone.'

Jesus, knowing that the net was closing in, 'no longer went about openly among the Jews, but went from there to the country near the wilderness ....' The wilderness is a potent biblical image: 'I will make a way in the wilderness,' said the Lord to the prophet Isaiah; after his baptism Jesus was led by the Spirit into the wilderness to be tempted by the devil; and now we see Jesus retiring to a place near the wilderness with his disciples.

The poor of Latin America in the terrible times of repression and death asked only that they be 'accompanied' on their way, and that their story should be told. In that spirit we can 'accompany' Jesus as he moves inexorably forward to his Passion. This accompaniment is a formula for Christian discipleship: the poor and marginalised of our world, those who were considered to be of no account, were Christ's priority, and we have been called, as Christians, to follow him.

### Thought for the day
Am I willing to accompany Jesus?

### Prayer
Father, let the gift of your life continue to grow in us, drawing us from death to faith, hope and love. Keep us alive in Christ Jesus, watchful in prayer and true to his teaching till your glory is revealed in us. Amen. (Week 16)

# Moire O'Sullivan
## Holy Week and Easter Sunday

*Passion Sunday*

### Express yourself

Is 50:4–9; Ps 118:1–2, 19–29; Ph 2:5–11; Lk 19:28–40

> *'Some Pharisees in the crowd said to Jesus, "Master, reprove your disciples", but he answered, "I tell you, if these keep silence, the stones will cry out".'*
>
> (Luke 19:39–40)

A rabble-rousing riot announces Jesus' arrival into Jerusalem, proclaiming the many miracles his hands have worked and broadcasting a defiant display of faith in Jesus as the Christ. It is all too much for Jesus' detractors as they attempt to silence the words and actions that would question their own religious and political authority. He may seem to get away with it for the time being, but this display must have hastened Jesus' untimely death less than a week later.

Like the Pharisees, there is often an inflamed irritation inside us too when someone else proclaims a different stance from our own or asserts a greater claim to the truth than ourselves. We want to silence them, make them admit they're wrong. We want our words to be voiced over theirs, so that all will believe our one-sided story. But, put in the others' shoes, we also know what it means to be silenced, to have our voices and views not respectfully heard. So therefore if one is free to express, then the other must also be given their turn.

Alien though it may seem to our own society, we also know however that there are many non-democratic spaces around the globe, often in less affluent countries, where this inalienable right of expression is not only denied but violently oppressed. The legislated illegality of multi-partyism, the crushing authority of monarchical rule, the oppression of religions, the outlawing of civil society groupings, the banning and dispersion of con-scientious protests: all around the world, there are still many citizens who live in fear of expressing their mere thoughts or beliefs lest they be punished. And yet, though they live in fear, they boldly dare to speak out: whether it is South Africa's anti-apartheid movement, Nepal's pro-democracy front, or Iran's proliferating blogs, people will always assert their freedom to say what they believe the truth to be. And just like in Jesus' time, there will always be stones who 'will cry out' even, and especially, if other voices are silenced.

### Thought for the day
Are you are free to express yourself without fear? Do you let others speak their minds?

### Prayer
Lord, you hear the voices that speak out in silence, you understand the cries of those who cannot show their tears. We join in one with all those who are suffering from such oppression, and pray that they may be granted freedom of thought, word and deed. Amen.

## Men and women of the world unite

Is 42:1–9; Ps 36:5–11; Heb 9:11–15; Jn 12:1–11

*'Leave her alone.'* (John 12:7)

Martha and Mary were close friends of Jesus. They welcomed him into their home, served him, listened to him, and valued him as a friend and confidant. With Martha and Mary, Jesus knew he could find rest, shelter and care. Indeed, Jesus knew and valued the many women who were in his company, respecting their roles, welcoming their solace, and saving them in times of distress.

It is with such thoughts in mind that we are hit with the sheer horror of the many women who continue today to suffer from the indignity of poverty. In direct contravention of Jesus' ways, he who fostered respect and attended to their needs, women are more than ever bearing the unequal brunt of our world's current share of hardship. We watch the burdened backs of women, carrying babies and bundles as they flee from civil strife, carrying water and wood home from miles away, carrying tools and seeds in the hope that the rains will finally water their land. And as we watch them, so they in turn watch their own children, who die too young for want of food and medicine, who miss out on school to work in the fields, their own children who grow up to continue the cycle of poverty that their own mother bore them into.

Women and poverty are synonymous. So tightly

entwined are the realities of being female and experiencing hardship that one cannot separate one from another in any efforts made to make our world a better place. In lifting up women so to push down poverty, men and women more than ever need to work together to create new synergies, new relationships not based on power but on respectful, mutual development.

Jesus himself upheld this model of equal relations, supporting Mary when suffering Judas' ridicule, speaking to the Samaritan woman at the well, rescuing the adulteress condemned to death by stoning. It is now up to us to follow his lead, so that the women of our world can be free, not only from inequality, but also from abject poverty.

### Thought for the day

Spare a thought today for the poorest women in the world who do not have our modern conveniences at their disposal.

### Prayer

Lord, at the beginning of time, you created male and female in your likeness, equal in beauty and stature. But our pride led us to suffer from our desire to rule over each other.

Help us to regain our balance, to respect and value our differences, and to recognise our mutual strengths so that men and women can live together again in harmony. Amen.

## Life out of death

Is 49: 1–7; Ps 71:1–14; 1 Cor 1:18–31; Jn 12:20–36

*'Now the prince of this world is to be driven out.'*

(John 12: 31)

The horror of holy week is revealed. In no uncertain terms, Jesus foretells his imminent execution, blurting it out to Andrew and Philip who have merely come to tell him of the arrival of his guests. Knowing what is to come, anticipating the emotional and physical agony that his captors will inflict, Jesus is already suffering before the first shackle has even been placed.

There will always be suffering in our world. Disasters will happen; death will steal our lives and loves away. But what is inexcusable is the suffering that we ourselves inflict on our own fellow humans, the terrible deeds and denials that litter our history because of our attempts to dominate one another. Whether it is inner city racism or sectarian violence, whether it is picking on a younger sibling or failure to respect our spouse, we all have seen or played a part in making another suffer for the sake of our own self-esteem.

Despite this reality, all of us, regardless of race, colour, sex, language, religion, opinion, origin or birth, are born with inherent respect and worth as human beings and children of God. No one can take this away from us, even if some may try. And it is only in recognising our God-given dignity that a foundation can be laid for the establishment of true and lasting freedom, justice, and peace within our world.

Fortunately Jesus understands and tries to tell us today that horrific acts of suffering, such as his own impending death, can serve as a catalyst for profound and positive change. The forgiveness that comes when a sectarian divide is healed, the humility and understanding learnt when a couple reconcile: these are fruit borne out of seemingly irreparable deeds. However, what we must ensure in turn is that this fruit does not itself rot and wither away. Rather, we need to safeguard these hard learnt lessons, so that no one else need suffer or die before we understand the inherent worth of the lives of others.

### Thought for the day
We may not kill the body, but do we kill the spirit of others by failing to respect them on the basis of their race, colour, sex, language, religion, opinion, origin, or birth?

### Prayer
Lord, we entrust to you all those who are suffering at the hands of others.

We also bring to you their captors who are inflicting such pain.

Hold and guide them all so that true reconciliation and respect may prevail.

May we too have the courage to promote and protect the virtues of freedom, justice and peace so that dignity for all is attained. Amen.

## Wednesday of Holy Week

### Betrayal of the innocents

Is 50:4–9; Ps 70; Heb 12:1–3; Jn 13:21–32

*'One of you is going to betray me.'* (John 13: 21)

Betrayal: the knife in the back from a trusted associate and confidant, Judas Iscariot. The severing of an unwritten pledge of trust and of respect between two friends. Betrayal: a small and almost inconspicuous event, which hurriedly precipitates Jesus' arrest, trial and murder.

And although a seemingly small betrayal can evidently manifest substantial consequences, betrayals weave their way through our lives with surprisingly nonchalant ease. It is made even the more serious when nation states, the pillars of our political world, renege on agreements and declarations that are supposed to uphold basic human dignity and protect our world for future generations.

Such betrayals by nations are most evident when it happens to those who are the weakest and most in need of our care and protection, that is, when it happens to our children. Though our world has agreed on the importance of protecting our children, and our elected leaders have added their signatures to documents to say the same, children around the globe continue to be neglected, abused, exploited, and hurt by the very same who are meant to be their protectors. Such is our world that a minor difference in latitude and longitude can mean a major difference in a child's access to health, shelter, education, water, play, self-expression, and freedom. And so we continue to witness child labour, child pornography, infant mortality, and child soldiers where promises of schooling, protection, health and peace were assuredly given. Their hopes for a happy childhood were put in us, and we have sadly betrayed their trust.

But we must realise that we can provide a better world for the next generation. We can help those nations, especially those who are still developing their potential, to truly uphold their commitments for their children. We, who have the means and resources to help, can assist poorer countries to provide resources for their little ones.

Jesus was innocent. He was also betrayed. Let us not betray even more innocent lives when we know how and have the resources to protect all of the world's children today.

### Thought for the day

Parents, do you protect your children and help them to grow? Kids, do you respect your family, friends and communities and thank them for their care?

### Prayer

Lord, you said, 'Let the little children alone, and do not stop them from coming to me; for it is to such as these that the kingdom of heaven belongs' (Matthew 19:14).

May your love for children become manifest in our hearts, so that we may never betray their innocent trust, but rather help them to grow in health and wholeness. Amen.

# Maundy Thursday

## Scrubbing away poverty

Ex 12:1–4, 11–14; Ps 116; 1 Cor 11:23–26; Jn 13: 1–17, 31–35

> *'You call me Master and Lord, and rightly; so I am. If I, then, the Lord and Master, have washed your feet, you must wash each other's feet.'* (John 13:13–14)

At the Last Supper tables dramatically turn, as Jesus kneels down to wash the dirt, grime and sweat from the feet of his friends. What follows is an extreme, even debasing, sign of service to his fellow companions on the way. But it also demonstrates an intimate tenderness and care, forgoing stature and status to do what needs to be done in order to prepare them for their final meal. In washing their feet, Jesus thus shows the true meaning of brotherhood, the unbiased serving of others to restore dignity to all.

Forty years ago, Pope Paul VI's encyclical letter, *Populorum Progressio*, called for this same service to be shown, calling developed nations to serve their brothers in their newly formed, independent states. Considering the deep scars that colonialism had carved, as well as recognising the North's superior resources and its evident power, it was considered not only their duty but a moral imperative to assist these emerging countries. Forty years on, the message still endures, but this time with an ever-widening gap between the rich and the poor on our planet. Though the calls for fair trade and aid remain the same, they have now been joined with additional woes, HIV/AIDS, terrorism, debt, corruption,

88

civil war, and environmental change adding to the litany of concerns to be addressed.

We, the citizens of the developed world, have registered our unease with the current state of global affairs. With our TVs beaming live images of ever increasing poverty into our homes, and our summer travels sometimes bringing us face-to-face with the poor communities, we now support the campaigns and buy fair trade. We also need to register politically, to bring into power those who can ensure that debt, trade and aid pledges are fulfilled, assuring them of our enduring support even if this dents our own pockets or demands changes in our lifestyle. The reality is that, like Jesus, we need to kneel down and humble ourselves so that the dirt of poverty can be finally washed away from the feet of our earth.

### Thought for the day
What else can you do in your life to make a difference to the lives of others, especially those who are poor?

### Prayer
Lord, you understand the complexities of poverty and the many barriers placed to prevent its demise.
You also know that solutions lie in drastic action, the kind that challenges and shocks.
Give us the bravery and humility to accept change and to sacrifice our ways so that the stain of poverty can be made history, once and for all. Amen.

## Tortured to death

Is 52:1 – 53.12; Ps 22; Heb 4:14–16, 5:7–9; Jn 18:1–19:42

> *'Pilate then had Jesus taken away and scourged. They kept coming up to him and saying, "Hail, king of the Jews!" and slapping him in the face.'* (John 19:1, 3)

Death becomes us all. Many hope and pray our deaths will be a peaceful affair, surrounded by loved ones and carers, relieved of pain and able to say our last goodbyes. Others wish it to come as a thief in the night, stealing us away without warning. Death too became Jesus. But what makes his death so horrific, what makes Good Friday so terrifying, are the moments that led up to his ultimate demise: for he was betrayed, beaten, scourged, interrogated, mocked and abandoned before the nails were finally driven in. He was tortured to the extreme, before death relieved him from the pain.

Poland's Auschwitz, Kenya's Nyayo House and South Africa's Robben Island are a mere trace of the many living memorials dedicated to humanity's inhumanity. They tell tales of state-sponsored torture dictating, controlling and abusing their fellow citizens, impoverishing them further, as if their countries' daily grind of poverty itself was an insufficient sentence. They reveal tricks of cruelty conjured up from the depths of depravity which aimed to silence their victims into submission. And though the words 'Never Again' ring through their now-empty corridors, we know it is happening now, again and again throughout the world. When will it end?

When will the cruelty Christ suffered appease our thirst for control and submission? When will our desire to degrade our own kind be shamed by the reality of the cross?

Even today, some of the perpetrators of these inhuman punishments will remember Good Friday, shake their heads and beat their breasts, and then return to their posts to continue with their crimes. But it will only be when these torturers deal with their own selves, their own betrayals, their hidden cowardice, their crowd-like anger and their blind obedience, and only when they begin to see Christ himself as their prey, that maybe the torture will end and Christ's sacrifice will finally have been deemed sufficient.

### Thought for the day
The torture that Christ goes through in the scriptures on Good Friday is happening again, right now, today. How does that make you feel?

### Prayer
Lord, we pray for the victims of torture.
Heal their wounds and soothe their pain.
Help them forgive those who have done them harm.
We pray also for the perpetrators.
May they understand the depths of the pain they have inflicted, take responsibility and feel true remorse for their actions, and make reparation for their sins. Amen.

## Hope in the midst of absence

Ex 14:10–31; 15:20–21; Rom 6:3–11; Lk 24:1–12

> *'On entering, they could not find the body of the Lord Jesus.'* (Luke 24:3)

Emptiness was all they found where a body was meant to be. They had wanted to see, touch, smell the expected decay, to no longer deny the death that had taken him away. Instead they only felt the empty void, a thousand reasons, questions, confusions resonating within. His body, gone, drove them into despair, desperation. And hope. For where he was not, pointed to a potential elsewhere. Thus, slowly, the emptiness within began to fill with perhaps a prophecy fulfilled. No proof to hand, only hope: but a hope strong enough to dispel the gloom and to fortify them with faith that they had not yet been overcome.

In Africa's slums, the emptiness is real. Behind the mud-caked walls of dwellers' shanty homes, no food, no water, no education, no healthcare rumbles within the stomach of their poverty. They are empty, hungry, tired and sick. They want answers to their woes, solutions for their daily grind, but their questions merely resonate within the stark emptiness of their hollowed out tombs.

And yet despite the dank existence within the world's abandoned grave, glimmers of hope sparkle. There are the unexpected greetings, smiles and handshakes to beckon you in, the rummaging for a stool to sit and drink the warmly welcoming tea, the queries for your health and latest news. From them, there is the gratitude for a new day and for the small mercies it brings. And yes, there are of course the tales of woe and sorrow: the lack of cash, the malaria relapse, the child not at school. But there is also real hope: that a neighbour will share some food, that the fever will go, that the landlord will relent, and that God will hear their prayers.

There is of course no proof that this fragile hope will be fulfilled. But, like the women at the tomb, though they see and understand the magnitude of all that is gone, they choose to hope and dare to believe that this emptiness could be a sign that salvation is close at hand.

### Thought for the day
Is there emptiness in your life? Have you thought of the opportunities this space can bring?

### Prayer
Lord, your presence brought light.
Your absence brought hope.
Help us to have faith that our disappointments and deficits are chances for new beginnings and sources of new life. Amen.

## The simplicity of life

Ac 10:34–43; Ps 117; 1 Cor 15:19–26; Jn 20:1–18

*'He must rise from the dead.'* (John 20:9)

This is what he died for: to bring life, so that we can live life to the full. But if this is his Easter gift to us, then why do we so readily embrace all that is life's antithesis? We hear of abortions, suicides and euthanasia. We speak of the negatives, the disadvantages, and all of life's drags. We wake up, commute, work, eat, and go back to sleep with a joylessness that wonders why we bother going on.

For Africa's poor, life is not easy: often there is no work, no money, no water, no food. But they know that joy itself is abundant and one of the few things in life offered for free. And so they avail of this bargain, always having time for a smile, a greeting, and some chatter. Inevitably, there may be a problem, but sure, life will get better some day.

The ebbs and flows of life from our earth are also warmly welcomed by Africa's poor. When a child is born, it is a gift that has survived the mother's hunger and pain, and brings new hope into the world. And when an old person dies, they say it is like a library that has burnt, the ashes carrying its knowledge away.

So why do the poor, who have least reason to laugh, embrace life so readily? Perhaps it is their awareness that today may be their last that makes life becomes more ready to be lived. Or is it that the poor behold the most precious secret of all: that, when we live more simply without excess, we become more grateful for life's little gifts and games? For when we have less, then the little we do gain is often appreciated so much more. When we have less, we are open to share so that others can give in return. So maybe our Easter journey has finally led us to this irony: that through grinding poverty and Jesus' death, we can be resurrected in simplicity and with the love of life.

### *Thought for the day*
Are you stopping yourself from living life?

### *Prayer*
Lord of life, at this time when life is cheap and loathed, may we be renewed in the Easter mystery of loving life, uncluttering our homes and hearts to discover the wonder of life's simplicities. Amen.

## About CAFOD

CAFOD is the Catholic Agency for Overseas Development. It is the official overseas development and relief agency of the Catholic Church in England and Wales. CAFOD has been fighting poverty in developing countries since 1962.

CAFOD believes that all human beings have a right to dignity and respect, and that the world's resources are a gift to be shared equally by all men and women, whatever their race, nationality or religion.

CAFOD is a member of the Caritas International Federation, a worldwide network of Catholic relief and development organisations.

CAFOD raises funds from the Catholic community in England and Wales, the UK government and the general public so that it can:

- promote long-term development, helping people in need to bring about change for themselves through development and relief work.
- respond to emergencies, providing immediate help for people affected by conflict or natural disasters.
- identify the causes of poverty and raise public awareness of them, encouraging supporters and the public to challenge the structures, policies and attitudes that reinforce inequality.
- speak out on behalf of poor communities, explaining the underlying causes of poverty and challenging governments and international bodies to adopt policies that promote equality and justice.

- promote human development and social justice in witness to Christian faith and gospel values.

### *Enacting Gospel values*

CAFOD's work is one of the ways in which the Church expresses and enacts its belief in human dignity and social justice.

It is inspired by Scripture ('to bring good news to the poor,' Luke 4:18), by Catholic Social Teaching and by the experiences and hopes of the poor, marginalised and often oppressed communities it supports.

It works to enact Gospel values – within and beyond the Church – including:

- concern for our neighbours and the wellbeing of future generations
- serving the common good to enable everyone to develop equally
- fighting for social justice and ensuring everyone's basic needs are met
- acting on the basis of need, not greed, and acting in solidarity with those living in poverty
- promoting the values of human dignity, community, stewardship and the integrity of creation.

CAFOD puts into practice the solidarity and communion for which the Church stands, and strives for a world built on interdependence, mutuality and sharing, where exclusion, exploitation and greed do not exist.

Website: www.cafod.org.uk

In 1945, the British and Irish churches created Christian Aid to put faith into action amid the ruins of a horrific war. Sixty years on, we work with church partners, the ecumenical family and sister agencies as well as with alliances of other faiths and secular groups which share our passionate determination to end poverty.

Christian Aid works wherever the need is greatest – irrespective of religion or race.

Because we believe in strengthening people to find their own solutions to the problems they face, we support local organisations, which are best placed to understand local needs. We also give help on the ground through 16 overseas offices.

Christian Aid Week each year is the largest house-to-house collection in the UK, with the involvement of over 300,000 volunteers and 20,000 local churches and committees.

We strive for a new world transformed by an end to poverty and we campaign to change the rules that keep people poor.

### *Our values*

The essential purpose of Christian Aid is to expose the scandal of poverty, to help in practical ways to root it out from the world, and to challenge and change the systems which favour the rich and powerful over the poor and marginalised.

*Put life first*

We believe that all people are created equal, with inherent dignity and infinite worth. Individual human needs must always come first, ahead of dogma, ideology or political necessity. We know that each one of us, in all our diversity and varied talents, can make a real difference in the battle to end poverty and injustice.

*Struggle for justice*

Poverty is a condition created by an unjust society, denying people access to, and control over, the resources they need to live a full life.

So we take the side of poor and marginalised people as they struggle to realise their civil, political, economic, social and cultural rights.

We believe in the just and sustainable use of the earth and its resources, so that the greed of one generation will not create poverty for the next.

*Speak out courageously*

We have a duty to speak out and act with conviction to challenge and change the systems that create poverty.

Christian Aid always remains independent of governments and other powerful institutions. We work to educate and mobilise people from all kinds of backgrounds to build a global movement which can change the course of history.

*Test everything against experience*

We know that poor people are the true experts on the nature of poverty, and our work is shaped by their voices and concerns.

In a spirit of humility, we try to learn from our own mistakes and from the experience of those we work alongside, to improve the impact of our work.

We know that lasting solutions can never be imposed on communities from the outside.

*Work together with others*
All our work is based on the spirit of cooperation and partnership. We help to build a world free from poverty through inter-faith and intercommunity dialogue and cooperation.

We nurture the talents, commitment and energy of all our supporters, volunteers and staff. Together we uphold a commitment to honesty, mutual respect, accountability and diversity.

### Towards a new earth
For Christian Aid this is a time to act upon our dream of a new earth on which we all stand equally, to renew our faith and hope, to reaffirm our commitment to the world's poorest communities, and to promote the dignity and rights of people throughout the world.

Website: www.christian-aid.org.uk